VIKING
BATTLE FOR ASGARD

D0731908

THE DAWN OF RAGNAROK

The darkest of times has arrived in Midgard. Hel, queen of the underworld, has turned against the forces of Asgard. She has opened the gates and unleashed an army of demonic minions, threatening to overwhelm everything in their path.

Many Viking towns have already fallen to this scourge, but the people have not been abandoned by their gods. Freya still has the strength to choose her own champion and face Hel. The time of ice and fire may yet be pushed back, and hope itself has not been extinguished.

ONE MORTAL STANDS IN THE PATH OF DESTINY

Freya's champion is the warrior Skarin. A man of immense strength, skill, and bravery, he is thought to be a cursed soul by some. But fate being what it is, Skarin must take up his weapons and fight beyond his mortal stature. Ignoring pain, suffering, and death itself, his task is to lead the Vikings and retake Midgard.

Skarin will face many challenges on this path. Thousands of Hel's demons are ready to fight him. They have no fear or interest in their own preservation, and they already possess many key locales throughout the land.

To defeat them, Skarin must save other Vikings and prepare them for war. Using his skills in battle, he can lead the charge against Hel while strengthening these allies. Tremendous battles await, in which dragons will be rallied to the cause, and untold horrors loom in the shadows to thwart the fate of man and god alike.

FREYA'S AID

Freya can bring Skarin back from death, but he needs even more assistance to defeat Hel. This tome is one more tool in Skarin's arsenal. These pages contain maps of Midgard, battle lore for all the weapon moves and magics that Skarin can exploit, and wisdom to help him succeed in warfare. With this guidance, Skarin can fulfill every achievement in the name of Freya and discover untold riches.

This knowledge was handed down by warriors who preceded you and found their glory. Their tactics and your bravery are the last defense against Midgard's destruction—do not falter!

LEARNING THE MOVES OF BATTLE

Skarin has mastered many of the basic skills of war, but he still has much to learn. Consult this chapter to find out what Skarin can do and how to control the flow of combat during skirmishes and large-scale battles.

XBOX 360 CONTROLS

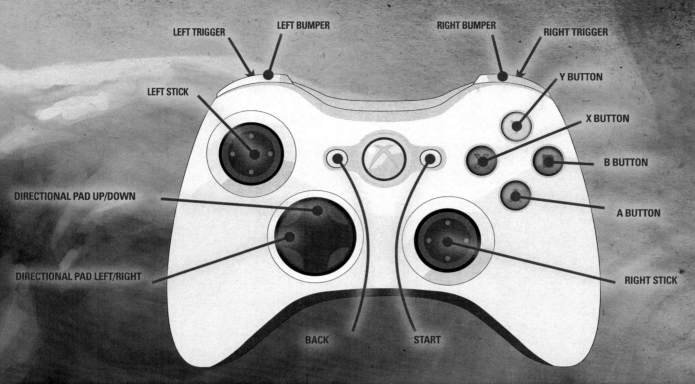

LEFT TRIGGER · LEFT BUMPER · RIGHT BUMPER · RIGHT TRIGGER

LEFT STICK

Y BUTTON

X BUTTON

B BUTTON

A BUTTON

DIRECTIONAL PAD UP/DOWN

DIRECTIONAL PAD LEFT/RIGHT

RIGHT STICK

BACK · START

CONTROLLER COMMAND	UNSHIFTED STATE	RAGE MODE
D-Pad	Not Used	Not Used
Left Stick	Player Movement	Player Movement
Right Stick	Camera Control	Camera Control
A Button	Fast / Light Attack	Fast RAGE Moves (Multiple Taps)
B Button	Focused Activity	Not Used
X Button	Slow Attack (Press and Hold for Super Strength)	Slow RAGE Moves (Press and Hold for Biggest Available)
Y Button	Jump	Not Used
Left Trigger	Block	Block
Right Trigger	Magic	Power Selection
Left Trigger + Y Button	Dodge	Dodge
Left Bumper	Rage Mode	Rage Mode
Right Bumper	Inventory Selection	Inventory Selection
START Button	Options	Options
BACK Button	Open Map / Inventory / Messages (Standard Play) or Freya Cam (Battle)	Not Used

CONTROLLER COMMAND	POWER SELECTION	INVENTORY SELECTION
D-Pad	Not Used	Change Target for Projectile Weapon
Left Stick	Player Movement	Player Movement
Right Stick	Camera Control	Camera Control
A Button	Not Used	Use Health Potion
B Button	Enable Fire Power (Region Buff)	Throw Flame Pot
X Button	Enable Ice Power (Region Buff)	Throw Throwing Axe
Y Button	Enable Lightning Power (Region Buff)	Not Used
Left Trigger	Block	Block
Right Trigger	Not Used	Not Used
Left Trigger + Y Button	Dodge	Dodge
Left Bumper	Not Used	Not Used
Right Bumper	Not Used	Not Used
START Button	Not Used	Not Used
BACK Button	Not Used	Not Used

L2

L1

SELECT

START

R2

R1

TRIANGLE BUTTON

SQUARE BUTTON

DIRECTIONAL PAD UP/DOWN

CIRCLE BUTTON

X BUTTON

DIRECTIONAL PAD LEFT/RIGHT

LEFT STICK / L3

RIGHT STICK / R3

Controls

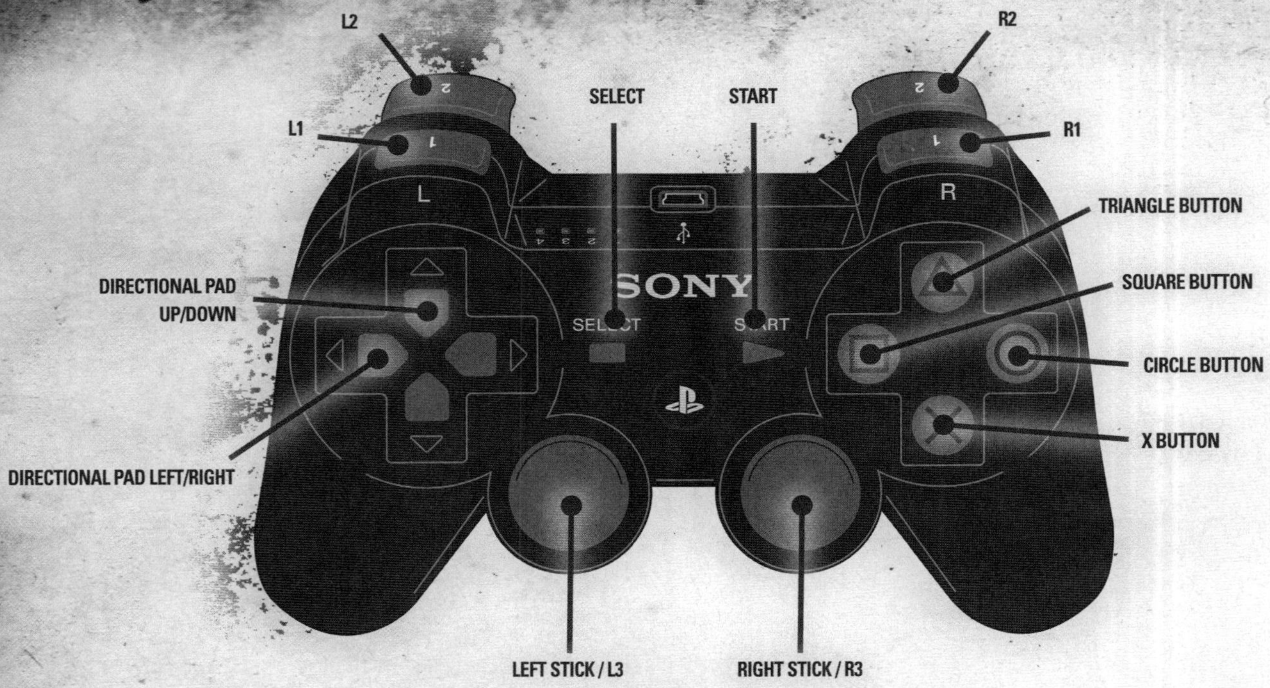

CONTROLLER COMMAND	UNSHIFTED STATE	RAGE MODE
Left Stick	Player Movement	Player Movement
Right Stick	Camera Control	Camera Control
D-Pad	Not Used	Not Used
X Button	Fast / Light Attack	Fast RAGE Moves (Multiple Taps)
Circle Button	Focused Activity	Not Used
Square Button	Slow Attack (Press and Hold for Super Strength)	Slow RAGE Moves (Press and Hold for Biggest Available)
Triangle Button	Jump	Not Used
L1	Rage Mode	Rage Mode
R1	Inventory Selection	Inventory Selection
L2	Block	Block
L2 + Triangle Button	Dodge	Dodge
R2	Power Selection	Power Selection
L3	Not Used	Not Used
R3	Centers the Camera	Centers the Camera
START Button	Options	Options
SELECT Button	Open Map / Inventory / Messages (Standard Play) or Freya Cam (Battle)	Not Used

CONTROLLER COMMAND	POWER SELECTION	INVENTORY SELECTION
Left Stick	Player Movement	Player Movement
Right Stick	Camera Control	Camera Control
D-Pad	Not Used	Change Target for Projectile Weapon
X Button	Not Used	Not Used
Circle Button	Enable Fire Power (Region Buff)	Use Health Potion
Square Button	Enable Ice Power (Region Buff)	Throw Throwing Axe
Triangle Button	Enable Lightning Power (Region Buff)	Throw Flame Pot
L1	Not Used	Not Used
R1	Not Used	Not Used
L2	Block	Block
R2	Not Used	Not Used
L3	Not Used	Not Used
R3	Centers the Camera	Centers the Camera
START Button	Not Used	Not Used
SELECT Button	Open Map / Inventory / Messages (Standard Play) or Freya Cam (Battle)	Open Map / Inventory / Messages (Standard Play) or Freya Cam (Battle)

COMMAND EXPLANATIONS

MOVEMENT

Push the analog stick gently to move Skarin at a slow pace, or push the stick fully in one direction to move Skarin as fast as he can go. You can move forward, backtrack, or dash to either side.

Skarin moves much slower if you block and continue moving. He maintains a defensive posture and knocks aside normal attacks from his front or flanks. However, he can't outrun his enemies in this stance. Blocking while moving is useful when you need to reposition Skarin without exposing him. It's also a good way to keep him facing forward. Normal movement to the left or right causes Skarin to turn and face the corresponding direction. Blocking movement gets Skarin to sidestep, so he keeps his eyes on whatever he's already facing.

When enemies are nearby, another type of movement is possible. If Skarin moves without being detected, he stays in a careful crouch and tries not to make much noise. You can clearly see that he is trying to be stealthy, and it works well if you keep Skarin out of view. This Viking has learned how to be quiet, but he can't avoid detection if an enemy looks directly at him. You'd pay attention to a huge Viking warrior stalking toward you, right?

Thus, you must maintain stealthy movement by creeping behind enemies and using objects to block their sightlines if they turn toward Skarin. Stealth is useful because it helps you manage the flow of combat. It's very easy to slice through enemies one at a time, especially when you get the first strike. It's not quite as simple if everyone sees you and rallies to your position.

VIEWING THE AREA

The right stick controls your view of the area. Press it from side to side or push up and down to get the best vantage point during your travels. Use the Options menu to flip the X or Y axis if you are more comfortable with inverted controls.

Notice that Skarin's movement is based on your viewing angle, not his direct position. Pressing forward tells Skarin to move away from the camera. Pressing backward moves him closer to the camera. It doesn't matter which way Skarin is actually facing when this happens.

Press in the analog stick to immediately snap the camera back into position behind Skarin. This is useful when you want to maneuver quickly but keep the view facing forward, often because of enemy threats. It also helps when you line up tricky jumps.

FAST ATTACKS

Fast attacks are a very good way to inflict damage and build up rage for making your special attacks. These moves don't leave Skarin exposed for very long, and there really isn't a downside to using them.

Each time Skarin lands a blow, he is awarded a rage crystal. Rage crystals are spent each time you make a rage attack. This is why fast attacks are much better for collecting rage; you can score two or three attacks in the same time that a single slow attack lands.

Chain a series of four fast attacks together to push enemies across the field and deliver considerable damage. Fast attacks don't have as much range as slow attacks, but they still hit from farther away than you might expect. If enemies aren't standing directly next to Skarin, he'll lead into his strike by taking a quick step.

SLOW ATTACKS

The longer you hold the button before releasing it, the more powerful Skarin's attack, up to maximum.

Slow attacks deliver more damage per strike. Plus, a fully charged blow can hit at very long range and open strike several enemies when that's possible. It's useful to prepare slow attacks at medium range, when melee troops can't exploit Skarin's vulnerability. As they advance, they end up taking your shots right on the chin.

The other way to use slow attacks is inside a chain. Hit an enemy once or twice with fast attacks, and use a slow attack at the end. This is only somewhat effective in the early game, but Skarin learns special moves to improve this method as time passes. Later, this technique becomes extremely effective for inflicting more damage without risking anything.

INTERACTIONS

Tap ⓑ to untie

Skarin can rip open cages, tear apart chest locks, and interact with other objects during his travels. A message appears onscreen when Skarin gets close to an object he can use. Press the interaction button once to begin operating the device, and tap the button quickly once you are told to do so. It's usually very intuitive, so you probably won't have any problems.

JUMPING AND CLIMBING

Skarin is a skilled jumper. He has so much strength in his legs that he can cross substantial distances and even leap over some of his foes. In a pinch, you can get Skarin to jump over groups of enemies and ditch past certain ambushes. It's extremely funny when it works, but don't rely on this too often. Enemies can knock Skarin out of the air, and he takes a fair bit of damage when this happens. He also loses his momentum and ends up on the ground, vulnerable to whatever attacks his enemies can prepare.

Press forward when you jump, and hold that position to help Skarin grab onto ledges. This extends the safe distance of his jumps. Press the jump button again while holding up to climb to the top of ledges.

Skarin can shimmy along the sides of a wall from which hangs. Press left or right on the analog stick to achieve this. It's sometimes necessary to hang over walls or to climb on vines when you want to reach a point that is too far for a leap.

If you see a small ledge, another trick is to have Skarin flatten himself against the wall and shuffle along its edge. This command is extremely intuitive; just have Skarin approach the wall, and he automatically starts his shuffle when he reaches a narrow ledge. Just move left or right with the analog stick to have him continue.

BLOCKING AND DODGING

Blocking is very powerful against light- and medium-strength enemies. Hold the trigger for this and watch as Skarin parries or blocks almost everything that comes at him. Any attack from the front or sides does not inflict damage while Skarin is blocking.

However, Skarin can't block an attack that comes at his back. Gently retreat while blocking to keep enemies in front of Skarin instead of letting them slip around to his back—groups of enemies *will* try to do this. Stay mobile and don't turn your back on anything.

It may seem tempting to run away from a large group of enemies. It's true that Skarin moves much faster when he isn't blocking. However, enemy sprinters can still outrun Skarin and hit him in the back. You can run from encounters you want to avoid when the enemies are still at long range, but turn and block as soon as opponents enter melee range.

Some attacks are unblockable, even when they originate directly in front of Skarin. Enemy champions and other heavy troops are so strong that their blows can't be parried. You must dodge these attacks. Hold the block button and tap the jump button to initiate a dodge. Do this when you see enemies winding up for a heavy strike! Later in the game, Skarin learns how to make counterattacks after a successful dodge, and that is extremely fun. It's effective too!

USING ELEMENTAL MAGIC

Skarin can't use elemental magic when he first begins his quest, but a little financial investment changes all of that. Seek the blacksmiths in major towns, and have them alter Skarin's weapons with elemental runes. The first tier doesn't cost much money, so you can make these purchases very early in the game.

Elemental magic has several functions. First, it improves the damage that Skarin's attacks inflict for a certain period. It also improves the damage that any nearby allies deliver when Skarin uses the magic. The more allies that are in range, the greater the benefit delivered to your troops. Thus, large battles are hugely influenced by your use and timing of elemental magic.

You gain the energy for casting this magic by killing enemies. Floating red clouds emanate from slain foes. Collect these clouds by walking through them. You don't get much for merely slapping down enemies with fast attacks. Instead, bludgeon enemies until they are vulnerable and kill them with finishing moves.

A finishing move is available when the enemy stops moving around and a button icon flashes over its head. Press the button and watch as Skarin performs one of many brutal actions to silence his enemy. You gain *much* more elemental power when you defeat enemies this way. This tactic also unlocks a few achievements over time.

Watch as the red bar underneath your health fills up. This represents the amount of elemental magic at your disposal. Activating fire, frost, or lightning effects depletes the bar slowly. You can't stop the process once it starts, and Skarin uses all of his power whether or not he is actually fighting. Thus, reserve elemental magic until you're in the middle of a very big fight.

Once Skarin is buffed with elemental power, he can channel the strength of the corresponding element into a massive attack. Press and hold both attack buttons, and point Skarin toward your most dangerous target. The effects are beautiful to behold. Save this power to bring down champions, bosses, and Hel's other prized servants. More about specific element powers is explained in the next chapter.

RAGE ACTIONS

Rage actions are a type of special move. Skarin learns these at various arenas found throughout the game. You must build up your supply of gold and spend it to learn special moves.

Trigger rage actions by holding the rage button as you make your attacks. Look below the health and magic bars; a number of crystals appear there as you hit enemies. You can build up five of these rage crystals at a given time.

Rage actions cost one to three crystals, and you trigger them with a variety of button presses. The ghosts of the arena explain each move, and you get a practice phase to master these actions before you have to leave.

Using a rage action depletes rage crystals, but you can renew them easily with several fast attacks. Don't be shy about using these moves, as they are extremely powerful and can defeat a wide range of enemies. Rage actions are usually targeted toward a specific problem, such as beating shield-bearing enemies, fast targets, and other troublesome foes.

USING YOUR INVENTORY

Skarin can purchase throwing axes, health potions, and eventually flame-pots. Use the inventory button to bring up a secondary menu during active play. As you hold down the inventory button, press a second button that corresponds with the item you want to use.

Throwing axes inflict high damage at range. A target is within range when the button icon appears over its head as you press the inventory button. If an enemy doesn't have an icon above its head, move a little closer and wait for the icon to appear before you throw your axe.

Health potions restore a small amount of health. These are most useful in battle because Skarin heals on his own when he isn't fighting. Keeping ample potions on hand costs quite a bit of money. It's wise to learn how to avoid using these too often. Keep them around for boss fights and other challenging encounters.

Flame-pots are not available in the early part of the game, but you can purchase them later on. These thrown weapons inflict damage over a wide area and cause a lot of trouble for enemies during skirmishes and large battles.

OPTIONS

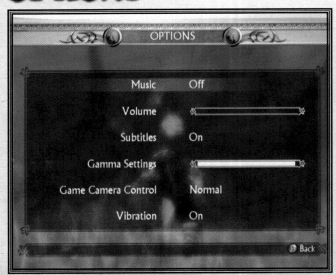

The Options menu pauses the game and gives you time to think, get up from the console, or do whatever you want to do away from the game. You can change your storage modes within the Options menu (should you wish to save to a memory card). You can also use this area to adjust the music volume, toggle the subtitle setting, adjust the gamma, disable vibration, or change the camera control.

YOUR MAP, MESSAGE, AND MOVE SCREEN

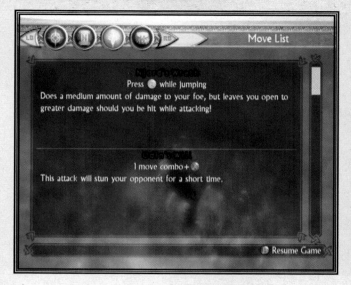

This menu has four sections. Initially, it shows either the regional map or Freya's view of the battlefield (during major fights). You can navigate inside these views. Highlight important objectives and set them onto your mini map.

When an objective is highlighted, you're given a list of things to accomplish there. This is extremely useful, because it lets you know if you've missed something in a region. The objective's color also provides information: blue sites are complete, red sites still have live quests, and yellow sites hold new information.

A slight yellow glow around an objective means that there is new information about the place or the nature of the task. Highlight the objective to see what's new, and the glow will fade.

The next tab to the right accesses your list of messages. If you've forgotten something that comes up in a quest, read this area for a reminder.

The third tab is a list of all special moves that Skarin has learned. Review this to ensure that you use Skarin to his fullest!

The final tab displays how much money Skarin carries and which items are in his inventory, including special quest items. It also shows all three elemental types next to your weapons. The adjacent runes fill in as you purchase them from the blacksmith!

Finally, there is a listing for Dragon Gems. These show up when you are involved in a large battle. Collect Dragon Gems by killing important enemies. You can then spend them to call down dragons and have them eliminate dangerous targets, keeping your ground forces relatively safe.

INVENTORY USES AND LIMITS

Item	Function	Limit
Health Potions	Restores a small amount of health when used	3
Throwing Axes	Single-target, ranged weapon	10
Treasure Chest Map	Reveals treasure chests on your mini map	1/Island
Urn Treasure Map	Reveals urns on your mini map	1/Island
Gold Bag Treasure Map	Reveals gold bags on your mini map	1/Island
Health Rune	Improves Skarin's maximum health	There are three unique Health Runes
Meal	Increases size of health bar by 50%, dropping with every hit Skarin takes down to his original 100%	1
Flame-Pot	Area-of-effect thrown weapon	10

TRAINING FOR WAR

Skarin's thirst for victory knows no bounds. Learn how to stalk the servants of Hel, to crush them when they are alone or in large packs. Discover the beauty of attack combos and special moves, and master the elemental arts. This chapter reveals the secrets of warfare to help Skarin win the battle for Asgard.

CHARACTER MOVEMENT

There is a lot of traveling to do before Midgard is freed. Use the in-game map to see where Skarin can travel. To make the process even easier, move your cursor around the map while the game is paused. This lets you highlight target areas. Click on these to lock the target into your radar, allowing for easier navigation.

In each region, some locations are hidden on the radar until you move close to them. Explore on foot and look for each area's odds and ends. This can be fruitful in several ways. Not only do you find the smaller caves and objectives necessary to complete the game, but you also stumble onto cash. The bags and urns of money littering the land are very important for purchasing equipment, special moves, and elemental runes. Exploration can make you rich!

LEYSTONES

You'll find a number of stone monuments, called Leystones, as you explore Midgard. These are very important for quick travel through areas you've already conquered. Leystones teleport you from point to point. You can travel between only those Leystones that you've already visited. Thus, you spend a lot more time exploring an area the first time through, until you find the Leystone, enabling faster travel.

There is always a Henge by Skarin's base camp in each region. This is where he returns if he is crippled in battle. Freya can bring him back from death, but she can't stop him from being brought down by a huge onslaught of monsters.

COMBAT MOVEMENT

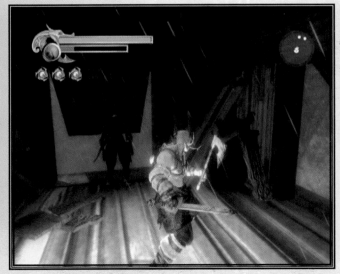

Skarin is no pushover when it comes to combat—after visiting the dueling arena, you'll be able to unleash devastating attacks on your Legion enemies! Good fighting is meant to be exciting and challenging, and tactical movement is a part of that. Skarin benefits from staying mobile during combat to keep his enemies where he wants them!

Stay attuned to where your enemies are standing. Don't leave archers or melee troops at your back. Use natural barriers, such as trees and walls, to keep foes from sneaking up behind Skarin. Circle around foes if they try to outflank you.

The worst scenario is to have melee opponents on multiple sides. Such a case leaves Skarin exposed and vulnerable, regardless of which direction he faces. This almost guarantees that he suffers damage during the fight, and the big guy can take only so much punishment before he falls.

We discussed blocking during movement in the previous chapter. It's a good way to walk precisely and avoid exposing Skarin's back to fast attacks. Use this tactic often and see how many more hits Skarin avoids or deflects. This doesn't cost you many attack opportunities, either. Skarin can go from blocking to counterattack without a noticeable delay.

In fact, Skarin can perform a pushing attack even when he's blocking. These fast pushes don't inflict much damage to your enemy, but they move the target backward. Use this technique to reposition foes, to buy time, or to knock victims off of cliffs and other high places. It's incredibly fun to watch powerful targets fall to their deaths from a mere push!

STANDARD ATTACKS

Skarin can beat a variety of enemies, even without special moves. His fast attacks chain together nicely, and his heavy attacks are good for punishing targets that approach slowly.

Early in the game, you use small chains of fast attacks to deliver most of your damage. You can't chain these if your first attack misses or gets blocked. But you can follow a successful fast attack with a few more. These chains inflict more damage than a single blow and they help push the enemy backward, allowing Skarin to cover ground. Staying mobile makes it harder for foes to close in on Skarin.

Once you visit the arena and learn some special moves, you can do even nastier things with attack combos. Just remember that performing any attack you've learned in the dueling arena costs you rage crystals, and you can perform the attack *only* if you have enough rage crystals to execute the move. Watch for Skarin to perform a fatality once you've defeated the enemy..

SPECIAL MOVE ATTACK COMBOS

Chain of Attacks	Name	Result
Fast, Heavy	Odin's Will	Jumping kick that throws enemies away from Skarin (short stun)
Fast, Fast, Heavy	Freya's Chariot	Higher damage attack with both weapons (medium stun)
Fast, Fast, Fast, Heavy	The Spear of Odin	Knocks enemies over, inflicts decent damage, and works well against shield-bearing enemies
Fast, Fast, Fast, Fast, Heavy	Valkyrie Strike	Another strong, damaging move against shield users

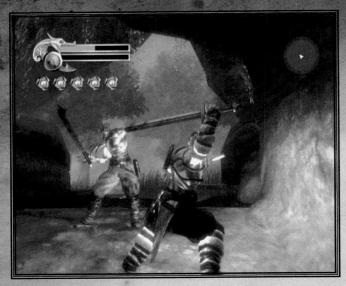

Moving the Left Analog Stick allows Skarin to attack multiple enemies during attack combos. Once you have engaged an enemy successfully with an attack combo, other enemies will not attack you.

Long attack combos also work well for solo enemies or targets that are at least temporarily isolated from their allies. Look for enemies that are somewhat separated from their group. This is also very effective if a single enemy gets behind you. Normally, that's a bad situation, but you can still exploit it. Turn around and launch a fast attack combo on the rear target. The combo pushes back the enemy and gives you some distance from the main group. Meanwhile, you rip the "crafty" enemy to pieces: a fitting reward for a back attack.

FINISHING YOUR ENEMIES

Normal enemies take only a few hits to bring down. They then start to waver and the finishing icon appears over their heads. You don't have to finish off all enemy types. Standard grunts, archers, and similar troops die on their own after a short delay.

However, finishing moves provide a big boost of elemental power. These attacks are also fun to watch. But if that isn't enough incentive, you *must* use finishing moves against some targets. Champions and other superior foes regain fighting status after a short period of vulnerability. You must close against these foes and use the proper button combinations to slay them before the opportunity expires.

Finishing off a normal enemy is as simple as pressing a button. You don't have to do anything special after you complete the slow attack. Just sit back and watch the dismembering goodness!

BOSS FINISHING MOVES

But bosses are different. Finishing them off requires sharp eyes and decent reflexes, at least for the first few times you attempt them. The button combinations to finish powerful enemies differ, and multiple presses are required. The first button icon that appears triggers the sequence, but you must remain attentive. Other button icons appear. Tap the corresponding button for blinking icons.

Stop pressing either button type when the icon disappears from the screen. But be ready to press a new button to continue the slaughter! If you make a mistake, your enemy will throw you from his back and you'll have to start again!

SPECIAL MOVES

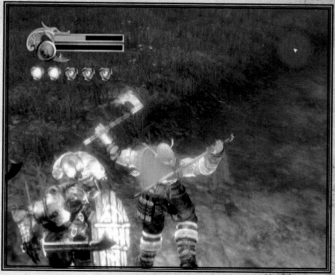

You learn special moves at the battle arena. Pay the ghosts there to show you how to destroy your enemies with better combos, jumping maneuvers, and rage attacks.

Most special moves are particularly effective against specific enemy types. A seemingly unimpressive attack becomes wonderful when you use it appropriately. For example, Thor's Hammer—a slow attack with a single rage crystal—seems worthless against enemy warriors. These heavy troops carry shields. They simply block Thor's Hammer, leaving you in no better shape than if you'd used almost any other attack.

However, try killing an enemy warrior with Baldur's Curse or Fafnir's Might! Shields don't mitigate these attacks. Likewise, use Thor's Hammer when a warrior has his back turned. Suddenly, you've scored a crippling blow with an attack that isn't supposed to be good against this enemy type!

Each special move serves a specific function. Learn them all! Try them all!

Category	Moves	Function
Jumping Attacks	Njord's Wrath, Hel's Fury, Odin's Doom	Burst damage while mobile, good against single targets and shield users.
Combo Finishers	Odin's Will, Freya's Chariot, The Spear of Odin, Valkyrie Strike	Bonus damage on combos and stun techniques.
Slow Rage Attacks	Thor's Hammer, Fafnir's Might, Might of Valhalla	Extremely high damage, good against armored or larger targets. Uses rage crystals.
Fast Rage Attacks	Baldur's Curse, Nidhogg's Strike, Curse of Fenrir	Defeats faster enemies well. Uses rage crystals.
Stealth Attacks	Fenrir's Bite, Baldur's Silence	Improves efficiency of surprise attacks at medium and close range.

ODIN'S WILL

COMBO ENDER: FAST ATTACK, SLOW ATTACK

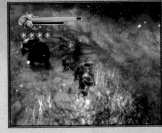

Odin's Will doesn't take much gold to acquire or much time to master. However, it's effective in the early and later stages of the game. Skarin makes a fast, standard attack and follows it up with a kick. This hit throws the target backward and gives you time to plan another set of attacks. Later combos provide higher damage and a longer stun, but they are also harder to set up and take longer to enact.

Thus, Odin's Will is always good for fast damage that pushes away an enemy. The attack itself changes Skarin's position; he drives into the enemy as he unleashes the combo. This is useful for getting away from enemies that are trying to outflank him.

Odin's Will is good against lighter targets. Archers, grunts, and assassins are suitable victims here. However, the combo's light damage makes it less attractive against warriors and champions. They're too likely to either block or absorb the hits, making it a poor choice compared to moves that provide greater burst damage.

NJORD'S WRATH

JUMPING ATTACK: JUMP + FAST ATTACK

Njord's Wrath is free. This attack doesn't inflict a ton of damage, but it's not very hard to set up either. Run toward a foe and leap into the air; perform a fast attack at your jump's apogee and plow into your victim, blade first.

Njord's Wrath's major drawback is that you can be hit out of the air without much difficulty. You're fairly exposed during the jump, and the payoff isn't very high. It delivers only a little more damage than a combo of two fast attacks. Plus, those fast attacks build up more rage crystals, and they're more defensive.

So, this move is painless to acquire, but it's not a substantial addition to your arsenal. You're usually better off using slow jumping attacks to start mobile fights. Those deliver a lot more damage and don't carry any increased risk or commitment.

THOR'S HAMMER

SLOW RAGE ATTACK: ONE RAGE CRYSTAL + RAGE ATTACK + SLOW ATTACK

Thor's Hammer is a gem in the early game. Get this attack as soon as you can, and practice it until you can use rage attacks without thinking about them. This is likely to be your first rage move, so learn its control system.

As a quick reminder, hold the rage button and tap the slow attack button once to use Thor's Hammer. You must have at least one rage crystal, but those are easy to grab; just hit enemies with your normal attacks.

Thor's Hammer inflicts quite a bit of damage, especially for a low-tier ability. You can wade through grunts by spamming this attack, and Skarin doesn't take much damage in the process. Grunts aren't very good at hitting Skarin while he's engaged in the leaping maneuver. They'll eat the blow and fall to pieces time after time.

Thor's Hammer is a great back attack against warriors. They can't block, and the full damage is nearly enough to kill them outright. Flanking shots are also a good bet. By its description, you might consider Baldur's Curse superior for killing warriors, but Thor's Hammer often wins out. Just find a way to avoid those shields, and watch the fun!

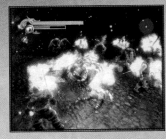

BALDUR'S CURSE

FAST RAGE ATTACK: ONE RAGE CRYSTAL + RAGE ATTACK + FAST ATTACK

This rage attack is very different from Thor's Hammer. It doesn't excel at pure damage, but it is almost impossible for enemies to avoid. Skarin lunges forward with great speed and pierces his target, avoiding their shields or dodging abilities. Though the description lists it as a good choice against warriors or assassins, it's really best just for assassin work. Warriors have decent health, and these single strikes don't lay them low quickly enough.

To augment the damage of Baldur's Curse, tack it onto the end of a fast attack combo. Slam into an enemy with two or three quick hits, and press the rage button to enable Baldur's Curse as a finisher. This adds to the combo's push, and it is a nice way to visually mix up your routine. Normally, people end combos with a slow attack, as those special moves are good for stunning victims. But Baldur's Curse is perfectly fine for variety and to use before you learn combo enders.

FENRIR'S BITE

STEALTH ATTACK: STEALTH + SLOW ATTACK

When enemies aren't aware of Skarin's presence, they don't use their shields or any other defenses. It's an ideal time to inflict major damage. Throwing axes are useful for killing at range, but Fenrir's Bite gives you an alternative that doesn't cost money. Creep up behind a target and look for the command to appear over its head; this indicates that you're in range for Fenrir's Bite. Press the slow attack button and watch Skarin close the gap.

This attack's subtlety is based entirely on your approach. Keep Skarin behind all of his targets, which isn't always easy. Use buildings to block sightlines, and watch patrolling targets to see when they are the most vulnerable. Patience pays for itself here, especially if you enjoy stealth kills.

FAFNIR'S MIGHT

SLOW RAGE ATTACK: TWO RAGE CRYSTALS + RAGE ATTACK + SLOW ATTACK, SLOW ATTACK

Fafnir's Might is a pure damage dealer that looks brutal and wonderful. You can use it as a stand-alone attack, or you can tack it onto the end of a combo. One of the best times to use it is when your first target falls back, ready to die. Skarin sometimes targets a new enemy with Fafnir's Might and kills it outright with ensuing hack. With the same investment you'd normally expend against one foe, you sometimes kill two!

The attack's animation is particularly nice, so it's a very stylish move. Its slow windup is the only major downside. If more than two or three enemies approach, the attack can be interrupted easily.

Rely on this special move during large battles. Nearby enemies are somewhat distracted, providing a target-rich environment. You can get away with using Fafnir's Might without continual interruptions. Champions are good victims too, as they have high health and require a serious pounding. Try fast attack + fast attack + Fafnir's Might, and watch the big game fall into your trap.

FREYA'S CHARIOT

COMBO ENDER: FAST ATTACK, FAST ATTACK, SLOW ATTACK

Freya's Chariot doesn't add as much damage to the end of a combo as you might like, but it has a much stronger stun effect than Odin's Will, your first ender. This special move knocks the enemy down and away, sending him tumbling. You then have plenty of time to regroup and pursue another target or follow up on your hapless victim.

Freya's Chariot is good for killing grunts and for taking down warriors, if you get a clean shot on them. The knockdown ensures that warriors can't reorient their shields against further attacks. However, you must be on the warrior's flank or wait until he is recovering from an attempted swing.

Avoid using this move against mighty champions. They are too big to push around, and Skarin is exposed as he finishes his combo. A champion is likely to counterattack, delivering an unpleasant amount of damage. Make sure that your targets are light enough to be thrown before you try combo enders against them.

NIDHOGG'S STRIKE

FAST RAGE ATTACK: TWO RAGE CRYSTALS + RAGE ATTACK + FAST ATTACK, FAST ATTACK

You'll fall in love with Nidhogg's Strike almost as soon as you learn it. This fast rage attack is a great improvement over Baldur's Curse; it lands more attacks, deals more damage, and is still fast enough to hit agile targets. You can wade through grunts, ambush warriors, nail assassins, or tack the move onto combos for high damage against strong targets, especially if you aren't afraid to take a little damage in return.

This move is as close to a "one size fits all" solution as you can get. It doesn't have many drawbacks, except that certain attacks are sometimes slightly better in specific situations. For example, champions are still easier to kill safely with short combos and slow rage attacks. *However*, you can kill them with Nidhogg's Strike.

HEL'S FURY

JUMPING ATTACK: JUMP + SLOW ATTACK

Hel's Fury provides a strong boost to your jump attacks. Njord's Wrath is barely an upgrade over a simple fast attack, and it exposes you to major damage if you time the maneuver poorly. Hel's Fury quickly dispatches light targets, so its risk versus reward is preferable.

Still, we don't recommend using Hel's Fury in the middle of larger fights when you're surrounded. Wait for enemies to be distracted. That lets you get off the ground safely.

Don't use jumping attacks against targets that are too tough to be killed by them. Skarin has a modest recovery time after he lands these hits, and it's not good to have the opponent turn the tables on him. Kill grunts, archers, and warriors with this, but avoid bringing it against giants or champions.

THE SPEAR OF ODIN

COMBO ENDER: FAST ATTACK, FAST ATTACK, FAST ATTACK, SLOW ATTACK

The Spear of Odin builds onto your combo ender repertoire. This time, you can complete a three-strike combo and smash your enemy back. The effect is supposed to be stronger against shield-bearing enemies, and you still enjoy the standard stun that comes with all combo enders.

Nonetheless, you can't often get this attack to work against its most obvious victims. Warriors are hard to nail with triple combos unless you surprise one from behind. And in that case, why risk the free kill with a combo? You could just as easily launch a vicious stealth attack or a slow rage attack and watch the warrior get hacked to pieces.

Honestly, the Spear of Odin has visual appeal and finesse, but it isn't an exceptionally powerful move. Purchase this later in your career, when you've mastered more of the essential special moves.

VALKYRIE STAMPEDE

COUNTERATTACK: DODGE + FAST ATTACK

Valkyrie Stampede is very tricky to perfect, but it isn't weak at all. The only reason most people don't use it continually is because they have trouble dodging. Dodging requires very good timing, and Valkyrie Stampede can be used only at the tail end of a successful dodge.

This sudden swipe inflicts moderate damage. Also consider that this is essentially free damage. The whole point of a dodge is to avoid an important enemy attack anyway, so instantly countering that is quite a perk!

You can use Valkyrie Stampede to dispatch grunts, but it's a minor waste. You can wade through grunts under many conditions, and staying defensive to wait for a dodge is awkward. It's better to use Valkyrie Stampede against enemies that you'd dodge anyway (e.g., assassins and champions).

All the same, practice this attack's timing during easy battles. Everything slows down when you're dodging, and it's possible to start a Valkyrie Stampede prematurely by hitting fast attack at the beginning of the dodge. Sure, this lets you begin the move, but you might get slammed in the face because your enemy is still finishing his first attack. Wait until the danger is past before you hit fast attack!

BALDUR'S SILENCE

STEALTH ATTACK: STEALTH + CLOSE RANGE + SLOW ATTACK

Baldur's Silence gives you a deadly stealth attack that's launched at close range. By the time you learn Baldur's Silence, you're likely to have a solid range of attacks against unwary foes. Thus, Baldur's Silence is more style upgrade than combat effectiveness boost.

That aside, getting close to your targets is risky. Axe throws from range or Fenrir's Bite are easier ways to kill foes when they aren't prepared.

Special Moves

ODIN'S DOOM

JUMPING ATTACK: JUMP + SLOW ATTACK

Your final jump attack upgrade raises the damage these burst strikes inflict. You can hop, kill, hop, kill, and so forth. It doesn't take long to recover, and you don't need rage crystals or any other energy type to perform these attacks. Parts of your enemies go flying in all directions—it's great fun to watch.

Odin's Doom is great in large-scale battles or against very small groups. It's least effective against clustered grunts that can knock you out of the air.

You might consider this attack suicide against champions, thanks to their high health. Surprisingly, this isn't the case. You can get into the air again soon enough to continue your aerial assault. As long as you reposition quickly and aim carefully, Odin's Doom can take down champions with some measure of safety.

Warriors can block a hit or two with their shields, but they also can't survive for long against Odin's Doom.

MIGHT OF VALHALLA

SLOW RAGE ATTACK: THREE RAGE CRYSTALS + RAGE ATTACK + SLOW ATTACK, SLOW ATTACK, SLOW ATTACK

Might of Valhalla is about as heavy as your attacks get. This is a shield shatterer. Use short combos with Might of Valhalla as a finisher to take down single targets that have protection or high health. You'll never be disappointed with this strategy. It looks impressive, it hits very hard, it destroys shields, and enemies that survive can't recover quickly enough to punish you.

It takes three rage crystals every time you use this ability, but that's why you use Might of Valhalla after short combos. Even two-hit combos give you almost enough rage for your special move. The fast attacks add a little damage to the combo. Champions don't last long in the face of this onslaught.

Don't waste this much power on archers, grunts, and their ilk. These light targets are too easy to bring down with other moves that cost less and don't require as much work.

VALKYRIE STRIKE
COMBO ENDER: FAST ATTACK, FAST ATTACK, FAST ATTACK, FAST ATTACK, SLOW ATTACK

Valkyrie Strike inflicts more than enough damage. It's part of a five-strike combo, so how could it let you down there? Still, this special move has a few downsides. Light targets don't survive long enough to let you enact the actual move. Archers and grunts are too soft, so they break your combo. Warriors have shields, so they slip in a block before you can land all four hits. Champions have the health, but Valkyrie Strike requires a long lead-in, and you have to risk your health while you rack up the fast attacks.

Thus, you end up with a special move that has real value but very few victims. As with a few high-end abilities, this is more a mixer to add variety and style to your fighting. Shorter combos are usually safer and are effective enough for your killing needs.

CURSE OF FENRIR
FAST RAGE ATTACK: THREE RAGE CRYSTALS + RAGE ATTACK + FAST ATTACK, FAST ATTACK, FAST ATTACK

Viking: Battle for Asgard's crowning special move is Curse of Fenrir. This visual gem is a marvel to watch. Skarin races between multiple targets (if possible), inflicting moderate damage to everything he hits. Enemies can't keep up with him, so the move is reasonably defensive. It's also an adaptable attack; Curse of Fenrir has just as many attacks even if there aren't multiple enemies in the area. This makes the move a good choice, whether you take on multiple grunts, assassins, champions, or almost anything else in Hel's legions.

ELEMENTAL ACTIONS

You take elemental power from fallen enemies. You don't use this energy as often as normal attacks or special moves. You usually reserve it for extremely important battles. Elemental energy can improve your damage or inhibit stricken enemies. It also buffs nearby allies and helps to win large-scale battles.

If you enjoy using elemental magic, perform finishing moves to kill all your enemies. Finishing move kills yield far greater elemental energy than other types of kills. All enemy kills provide at least one red orb, while fatalities provide three.

Elemental magic takes one of three forms: fire, lightning, or ice. Because you purchase the runes for this magic from the blacksmiths, you don't get all three types right away. It's better to lean on one of the three until you perfect it and then branch out into the other two.

Don't worry too much about this choice; there is plenty of money for all the special moves and blacksmith runes, so you can use everything in the game eventually.

Fire damages over time. Its buff sets your weapons alight and does the same for nearby allies. Enemies struck with flaming weapons suffer greater damage even after the initial strike, as the flames burn around them. As a special attack, you can unleash a linear burst of flame. It hits your target and inflicts high damage. Anything that comes too close is also struck and tossed aside. This makes fire a great option against grouped enemies in large battles.

Lightning delivers damage directly. Use it to improve your damage and that of your allies. The damage affects enemies immediately upon impact. Lightning provides perks against single enemies; each hit delivers the increased damage. Fire's buff doesn't stack to create larger and larger flames around the target; it simply renews their burning misery. Thus, fire is better against large groups, even before you use its special attack. Lightning does a better job against big game, such as enemy warriors and champions.

Lightning's special attack is similar in concept. It hits a single foe, making his life very bleak. The target is suspended in the air, unable to counterattack. Fire doesn't leave you too exposed to peripheral enemies, because they sometimes slam into the flames. Lightning doesn't hit anyone except your target, so enemy troops can easily outflank and attack you.

Of the three, ice has the most defensive buff. It doesn't deliver greater damage to targets, but everything struck is encased in ice and can't attack or block—wading through challenging enemies was never easier! When you're buffed with this, you can devour waves of medium-difficulty enemies. The ice special move is valuable, as it can stop all the enemies around you in one hit, rather than you having to hit them individually. This buys you time and allows you to shatter them all. Use ice if you're low on health and need to buy time.

RECOVERING FROM YOUR BATTLES

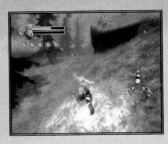

No matter how good you become, you still take damage There are just too many enemies to fight without making a few mistakes. Thus, there will be injuries. But there are ways to mitigate this problem, both in and out of combat.

During combat, you can drink health potions to help you through rough patches.

Away from combat, you start to heal on your own, so long as no enemies are in range. Break away for a few moments if you want to top off your health quickly.

THE UPS AND DOWNS OF HEALING

Healing Method	The Upside	The Downside
Resting	It's free!	Rest heals you only away from combat.
Health Potions	They work in combat and you can carry 3 of them.	These are very expensive, especially if you use them frequently.
Meals	They add extra maximum health and they aren't pricey.	The health lasts only until you take enough damage to negate the buff.

These methods are best used together, as with so many things about the game. Resting outside of combat is a no-brainer; it spares you from wasted deaths and saves you a great deal of money you'd otherwise spend on health items.

Health potions are probably the least impressive healing method. It takes a lot of money to maintain a supply, and drinking a potion requires active use during battle. Beyond that, they don't restore as much health as you might like. Consider health potions your last-ditch healing method, using them only in a boss fight's later stages, when you just need that little bit extra to make it through.

Meals pay for themselves many times over if you're good at avoiding heavy damage. When you purchase a meal from the shop, you consume it immediately. A meal increases the size of your health bar by 50%, but this drops with every hit you take down to your original 100%. A person entering a difficult and unfamiliar area might lose this boost within a few moments, so do your best to preserve each meal's health benefit.

One method that you can't fully control is collecting green energy from fallen enemies. Green orbs are dropped by any slain enemy when you drop below 30% health. However, only one orb is dropped, so if you don't pick it up before it disappears, you'll have to kill another enemy before another orb arrives.

Using the Map and Radar

Freya has given you great weapons, the will to continue beyond mortal capacity, and her sincere blessing. She has also given you her Brisingamen. The Brisingamen is the glowing talisman that hangs behind you. It contains your map and your current game-state. Its presence is shown at the top of the game screen; you can use it to track the whereabouts of items of interest in the nearby vicinity. In other words, its onscreen presence serves as a type of radar. You can use this to see objectives, explore the wilderness, and select destination points.

Freya also communicates with you through the Brisingamen. She discusses each location as you approach it, warning you against danger or simply providing background information about Midgard.

Naturally, the radar has less detail than the large map, but it is still useful. Purchase gold maps from the general store to reveal gold dots on your radar. This is a huge help in finding money throughout the land. Quest targets and important locations also appear on the radar.

The main map displays differences in elevation; the lighter regions are higher than the darker regions. If you can't find something that's displayed on the radar, try to find a way above or below your position to see if the item is located elsewhere.

Making and Spending Money

Money is essential for upgrading some your combat maneuvers. You must spend gold to acquire special moves, elemental runes, health items, thrown combat weapons, and other upgrades. Players who search thoroughly for money can upgrade much earlier than their rivals, and that makes the game easier and more entertaining.

It's wise to purchase all three treasure maps from the storekeeper. You can find some of the money that litters Midgard even without these treasure maps, but seeing the blips on the mini map makes a huge difference. You spot two to three times the number of items, especially as you wander through the wilderness. Many bags of gold are hidden under bushes or in other unexpected places. Buy the maps and watch the money roll in—they are worth the investment!

Determine your own priorities for spending money, as many of the choices are worthwhile. However, it's worth thinking about the long-term consequences of your choices before you spend anything.

Health items and thrown weapons are more useful in the later game. The early challenges aren't so fierce, and consumable items are clearly a short-term purchase. Getting special moves and elemental runes early in the game is a long-term strategy. These purchases are permanent; they make you stronger and more versatile in combat for the entire game, so it's nice to get these as soon as possible.

Once you've bought and learned enough moves and elemental attacks, you can make more and more short-term purchases during your shopping runs. It's always good to have a few throwing axes around. These are the cheapest consumable product. Even a single axe can deliver a fair bit of damage. They're great for ambushing enemies at range or from a different elevation.

For the most part, reserve health items for critical battles. Use them during long quests or in boss fights. Rely on skill and caution for survival, especially early in the game. This saves enough money to purchase more upgrades. It also encourages efficient combat that helps you in the later stages.

ARMY SCENES

Some areas can't be seized until you lead the warriors of Midgard into battle. The conditions for these fights are listed on the map. You usually have to gather a specific number of Viking clans before you can attack the location. Sometimes, there are additional goals, such as summoning a dragon or sneaking into the area to damage the enemy forces ahead of time.

One word of warning is to avoid these areas as much as you can before the battle. There are often hundreds of enemies nearby, and you can't take on all of them. Walking into Darkwater or other such towns can get you surrounded by Hel's minions. It gets hard to run, block, or survive, and the result is usually a painful beating.

BEFORE THE FIGHT

There are times you *must* enter these areas without your army. There are smart ways to carry out these infiltration runs. Don't walk in through the main gates! Your enemies aren't rocket scientists, but neither are they complete morons. Expect main entrances to be very well guarded. Look for small sections of damaged wall to hop over. Scout out the towns' perimeters to see what's there. Usually you can find some way to sneak in without facing the full brunt of defenders.

Once you're inside, hide behind buildings and kill stealthily whenever you can. Duck back when multiple enemies see you, and fight them away from the roads. This should prevent large groups from noticing the action and joining the fray.

Be especially vigilant against enemies that carry large horns. They sound an alarm when they see you, and the noise calls defenders to battle. It's a bad situation when that happens, and you might have to back off.

Stick to alleys and fringes of contested towns, looking for your goal. There are visual clues in these situations. Enemy portals shine with a fierce red glow, so they are easy to spot. Important enemy buildings are also large and imposing. Turn the camera around and pan it from side to side; don't break cover until you have a good idea where you're going.

SKIRMISHES

Often, you must fight small battles to liberate settlements and complete objectives. These fights feature a relatively small number of allies and enemies. They are also more straightforward than epic clashes. Skarin brings his allies into battle, and the two sides often push into each other for a short, ugly tussle. You don't see many high-quality enemy leaders, and there aren't as many surprises.

Use finishing moves as often as possible during these skirmishes. You need the elemental energy from these kills to stay buffed. Fire attacks work very well when targets are close together. Furthermore, using these elemental buffs keeps allied troops at their best. They kill Hel's creatures much faster, and that by itself can turn the tide of battle.

It's also nice to fight distracted enemies, and skirmishes are ideal for that. Some enemy groups rush toward you, but most of them focus on regular Viking warriors. Thus, they leave their backs exposed, allowing you to bring down armored and shield-bearing targets just as easily as simple grunts. Use heavy attacks and slower special moves to inflict massive damage, and don't worry as much about defense until the enemies turn their attention your way.

Watch for reinforcements as you lead the charge. Enemies pour into the battlefield from time to time, and it's not safe to get hit from behind by 20 angry grunts. Watch to see which areas the enemies use to enter the battle, and stay beside those locations or away from them entirely.

Also, try to stick close to your allies. You can survive on your own, but you can't buff as many friends or benefit from their distractions. There's safety in numbers, and it's much easier to overwhelm a lone hero.

EPIC BATTLES

Tricks that apply to skirmishes are still useful, and sometimes essential, in large clashes. However, you must integrate more factors into your strategy. Large-scale battles feature many more troops, and defensive structures often play a larger role. You also face more enemy leaders. You have to spend more time pursuing high-level enemies instead of helping your rank-and-file troops. Without your intervention, Hel's best champions and shamans can easily turn the tide against the Vikings.

Read the next chapter to learn about the individual enemies that constitute Hel's ranks. Specific moves and tactics work well against each. Once you master these tricks, it should be much easier to push the battles forward and give your forces the edge they need.

Specific enemy leaders are sometimes called out on your map. This is often the case for shamans. It's bad enough to have champions ripping into your Viking friends, but shamans present a dire threat without directly killing a single man! These bosses raise souls from the underworld to bolster Hel's army. You can't defeat a team that has infinite reinforcements, right? Thus, you must kill shamans as quickly as possible.

Use your map to see a wider view of the battle and access information about major targets. You can scroll between active points on the field, and this is also where you can call in dragon support. Each target costs a specific number of Dragon Runes to destroy. You gain dragon gems by defeating enemy bosses.

Not every boss is clearly identified as a target. After all, some of them are just big, tough guys who pose a threat to your army. They aren't all special or in command! But you can see them from a greater distance because they glow with red energy, the same energy that surrounds Hel's portals. Watch for that red glow and assassinate the leaders even if they aren't mandatory targets. This provides more dragon gems. In turn, you can kill entire enemy sections with dragon fire rather than direct combat. This saves Viking lives and allows your forces to concentrate on major objectives.

Use care as you plot a path toward your objectives. Don't push directly into the meat grinder that characterizes the battlefront. Look for side routes into the midst of your targets, hit them from their flanks, and maintain enough space to get around without fighting your way through every grunt with a chip on its shoulder. Sometimes flanking maneuvers are already clear; the scouting runs you make before battles are useful for highlighting the sneaky ways to get around. Use your experience in the area to avoid choke points and enemy ambushes.

MINIONS OF HEL

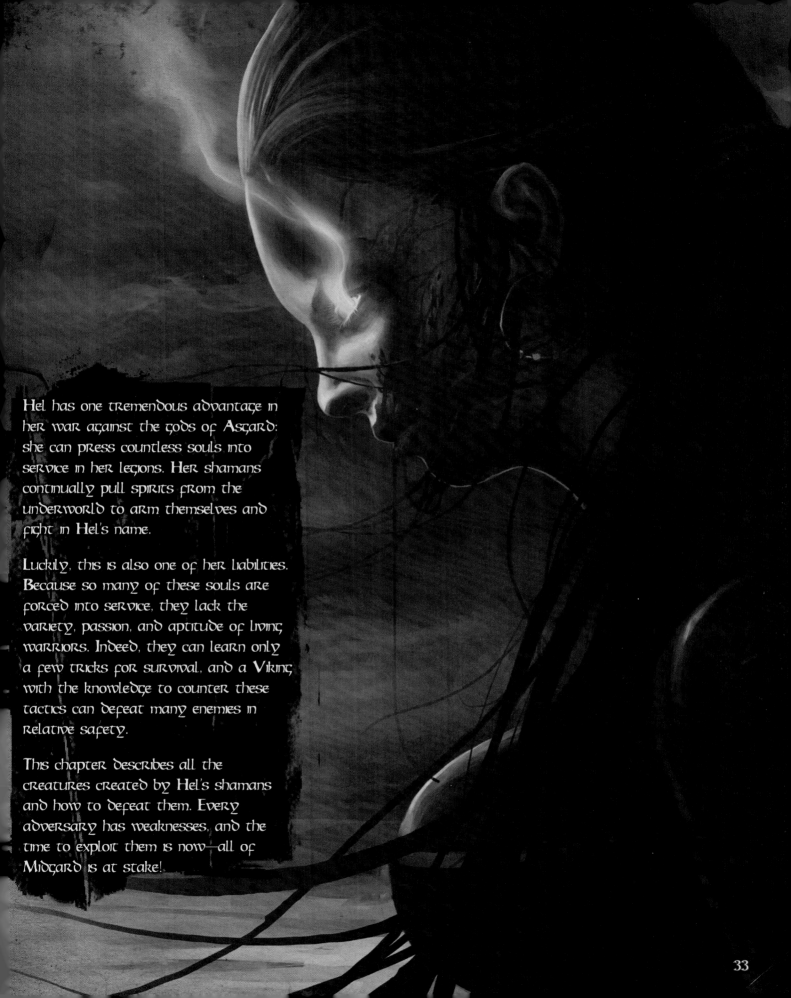

Hel has one tremendous advantage in her war against the gods of Asgard: she can press countless souls into service in her legions. Her shamans continually pull spirits from the underworld to arm themselves and fight in Hel's name.

Luckily, this is also one of her liabilities. Because so many of these souls are forced into service, they lack the variety, passion, and aptitude of living warriors. Indeed, they can learn only a few tricks for survival, and a Viking with the knowledge to counter these tactics can defeat many enemies in relative safety.

This chapter describes all the creatures created by Hel's shamans and how to defeat them. Every adversary has weaknesses, and the time to exploit them is now—all of Midgard is at stake!

Archers

Archers are one of the weakest troops at Hel's disposal. They have very little armor, they fight poorly in melee, and they can't take more than a few fast attacks before they succumb to Skarin.

However, archers are still very annoying, and they make life difficult when Skarin is beset by other troops. Archers stay up in guard towers or high on hills, firing their arrows at Skarin to disrupt and lightly wound him. This puts pressure on Skarin and limits his options.

First, keep Skarin's back away from the archers. Blocking can protect Skarin from arrows, but he can't block arrows that come at his back. Lure melee enemies away from their archer support and try to find safer places to dispatch them. Undersides of hills work well for this; buildings are also good for blocking archer sightlines.

Sometimes there isn't any adequate cover. Stay in a defensive position and wait for the archers to waste their shots. After the arrows are deflected, launch an aggressive series of attacks against nearby enemies. Dispatch them between waves of archer fire, and resume Skarin's blocking when the next volley is loosed.

Archers on the ground are very easy to dispatch. Block their attacks and slice them to ribbons. To get archers that are higher up, you can use throwing axes or approach the archers' position and coax them down. Like many of Hel's troops, archers sometimes put themselves in peril. They leap down and engage Skarin directly if he gets close enough.

Assassins

Assassins look very different from grunts, archers, and other members of Hel's Legion. These killers crouch and move close to the ground. They are agile and crafty, making sudden changes in direction and avoiding heavy attacks. Assassins use clawed gloves to carve into their victims at close range, and they inflict a lot of damage despite their diminutive frames.

Assassins aren't very common, but they make up for their modest numbers with nasty tactics. These attackers try to hide until their quarry gets close enough to ambush. They can leap onto a target's back and tear at its head and neck with impunity. Shake the movement stick to knock assassins off of Skarin. Follow this up with normal fast attacks or rage attacks that employ fast swings. Otherwise, the assassins can dodge and slip away to prepare more back attacks.

It's important to build up rage crystals when assassins are around. Assassins sometimes dodge fast attacks, making it much harder to defeat them quickly. That's why it's good to focus briefly on other targets to build the rage you need. You can quickly shift to a grunt, slice him apart with three or four fast attacks, and then use a fast rage attack to kill the assassin. It's better than taking down the assassin with only fast attacks!

BERSERKERS

Berserkers are not a common sight. As ground troops, they are superior to grunts and warriors but they occupy a notch below Hel's champions. Berserkers move into melee range, swing quickly, and inflict a fair amount of damage to their targets. They are tall, muscular, and don't go down quickly even when their enemies return the violence.

A strong defense works well against berserkers. Their attacks are fairly easy to block if you eliminate their supporting troops. Go after nearby archers and grunts for fast kills. Then play the block, counterattack, block game to defeat berserkers.

Berserkers are tough, certainly, but they aren't quite large enough to prevent Skarin from throwing them around. Combo-enders work wonders against these enemies. You can pile on the damage from the fast attacks, and then avoid reprisal by tossing the berserker away. Use the time that this stun effect provides to start a new combo or to attack other enemies before the berserker can return.

CHAMPIONS

These tall, armored troops lead waves of grunts into heavy combat. They are meant to be feared. Champions absorb massive damage before they fall, and they aren't shy about swinging their schlachterschwerts either. Those heavy blades are too powerful to parry once they're in motion. Even Skarin can't deflect something with that much force. Instead, master fast dodging; otherwise, champions are nearly undefeatable.

Fights against these enemies are a hit-and-run affair. Skarin must get in close, launch a quick combo, back off, and then dodge the champion's counterstrike. Some of the champion's attacks are single blade strikes. However, the foe also has a fast shoulder charge, which is very hard to avoid until you get used to it. And, on some occasions, champions start combos of their own. Don't get close when this happens. Just let the attacks run their course while Skarin stays back.

You must press a series of buttons to finish off champions. A champion is vulnerable when he visibly sags and starts to pant. A series of button icons appears over its head! Press the corresponding buttons in the correct order. Tap the blinking button icons, hold the ones that are static, and watch the champion fall!

Be ready for the match to continue if you mess up the combo by taking too long or pressing the wrong button. The champion recovers and starts to attack Skarin again. It then takes several hits to put the champion back into a vulnerable state.

Elemental magic is a superb way to kill champions. Ice is especially good for this because it can freeze the large fellows and give Skarin an opportunity to kill them outright! You don't have to go through the long button combination to finish them off.

Giants

You don't see Giants early in the war, but you can bet that Hel is reserving them for important battles. These humongous monsters are very dangerous because of their strength and tenacity. Many varieties of giants roam Midgard, but the type that Hel's Legion employs is somewhat specific. These brutes are over 15 feet tall and have long, powerful arms. They try to swipe their enemies aside or grab them outright. Their leg stomps shake the ground fiercely and make it hard for people to keep their footing.

Skarin can kill these enemies by whittling them down. Come in for a fast attack or two then back away with a dodge. Let the giant commit to a failed attack, and then rush back in for a fast attack and a level-two or -three slow rage attack. That registers major damage, and the process is very repeatable.

Use lightning to raise your damage if possible. You can't freeze giants, and fire isn't quite as effective as you'd like. Beyond that, unleashing lightning's power is enough to lift even giants into the air, so you can wound them and earn some respite if things get desperate.

When a giant is wounded enough, you must use a series of button combos to kill it. It's a lot like finishing off a champion, but there are stages of moves. Engage the second and third series from the injured giant's rear. They stay bent and exposed for some time, so you don't have to rush into this. Get ready and have at it! The button sequences are very similar, unlike with champions. So, once you've killed a giant, you'll see major improvements in your next fight with one!

GRUNTS

Grunts are the rank-and-file troops in Hel's army. They have minimal armor and simple blades, but they rarely appear in small groups. Expect to face countless grunts in the larger battles. Substantial teams of grunts guard even the smaller locations, and Skarin must wade through those without much help.

Thus, you must kill grunts rapidly without exposing Skarin to damage. Several special moves are good for this task. Thor's Hammer is one of the first that you learn. It can dispatch a grunt in a single blow! A chain of three fast attacks also gets the job done.

Use tactical positioning to buy Skarin time. It's better for a group of grunts to come toward you in a line rather than a pack. Back off from a cluster of enemies and move around buildings, trees, or any other obstacles. This forces the grunts to break up their formation slightly. Use a heavy attack, like Thor's Hammer, each time one of the enemies pokes its head around the corner. Doing this makes a group battle much easier to win without continually getting pecked by grunts on your flanks.

When conditions force you into a stand-up fight, be ready for continual blocking and repositioning. Shuffle to the side to keep the enemies on one side, and launch your attacks between the volleys of blows. This isn't as easy as duck-and-cover fighting, but suitable shelter isn't always available.

Horn Blowers and Elite Grunts

There are two types of special grunts that you will encounter. Horn blowers are armed like normal grunts, but they have a special role in the field: they rally forces together. Horn blowers call for help as soon as they spot Skarin, and this can get you into serious trouble. Use stealth attacks, throwing axes, or an onslaught that's rapid enough to cut their calls short!

Elite grunts are the other rare type. These foes can't take many injuries before they succumb, but they dish out damage at a frightening rate. Elites dual-wield, carrying an axe in each hand, and they've learned how to get both of them up to full speed. Use defensive fighting to buy Skarin time, and perform a fast attack or two in response to an elite grunt's flurry.

SHAMANS

Shamans are even creepier than most of Hel's minions. They look more like monsters than people, and their dark magic shrouds them in a field of protection.

But these enemies must be killed. They are Hel's greatest asset in battle. Without her shamans, she can't bring new troops into major battles. So go after every shaman you see. These eldritch casters are often surrounded by a series totems. You must destroy the totems to expose the shaman. That's not as easy as it sounds.

Grunts continually pop into Midgard through these totems, so you must divide your attention between attacking the totems and eliminating new grunts. Use fast attacks on the incoming grunts to kill them and build rage. Then unleash slow rage attacks on the totems to deliver high damage.

Once they take enough damage, the totems break and turn into pillars of flame. Don't take too long destroying the remaining totems; shamans continue summoning grunts, and they eventually restore their damaged totems. Break them and kill off the shaman before he can restore his shield.

Ironically, the final blow against an exposed shaman is the easiest part of the fight. The shaman isn't very good at protecting himself from physical attack, and he is taken aback at his shield's collapse. Simply close on the shaman and use a finishing move to rip him asunder.

WARRIORS

Warriors are upgraded Legion foot troops. They don't have special powers, but they take a lot more damage than grunts, especially if you attack them from the front. Warriors wear heavier armor and carry large shields to block Skarin's attacks. It's wise to respect these guys, because they're a nasty threat when you take them lightly.

Their shields are good for absorbing damage, but they also stop Skarin's combos. Warriors can block an attack and counter with a swing of their own. This isn't guaranteed to hit, but it throws off your timing and makes the fight harder, especially if a few grunts are also nearby.

Several tricks can help you avoid this. First, attacking warriors from behind is very effective. They fall with only a few hits. One slow rage attack should be enough by itself, letting you avoid the shield issue altogether! A stealthy approach lets you ambush some warriors, facilitating back attacks. You can also rush to their flanks during a fight and attempt to score cheap shots, even against targets that see you. Hurling axes at patrolling warriors' backs is also efficient.

Fast rage attacks work in direct combat. Many are designed to bypass shields by striking the victim quickly. Several of these attacks can shred a warrior. The later-stage slow rage attacks are also wonderful. These moves break the shields instantly and give Skarin free rein to cut warriors in half.

Try the following maneuver for fun: Back away from the fight and prepare a full-strength slow attack. The warrior engaging Skarin eats a combo of heavy hits that's often strong enough to rip his shield to pieces. You can use this method to eviscerate warriors you encounter early in the game. But flanking attacks and fast rage attacks are ideal for later fights, against warriors that carry stronger shields.

The earliest warriors you encounter have wooden shields. It doesn't take many attacks to rip these to pieces. After you smash their shields, these warriors find it difficult to defend themselves, and everything wounds them equally well. However, warriors in Galcliff and Isaholm use metal and stone shields instead. These shields withstand so much damage that it's far better to use shield-breaking attacks or high-tier fast rage attacks.

Remember to use Skarin's blocking prowess to protect him from warrior swings. These enemies are slow to begin their strikes, but once they start moving you should expect multiple attacks to come your way—just like your own fast combos. Keep up your defense until the warrior tires, then counterattack without fear.

THE EPIC OF SKARIN

Hel already has control over most of Niflberg, Galcliff, and Isaholm. With this much power over Midgard, she can hope to take her war to into Asgard as well. She must be stopped, but her Legion is strong and fearless. It's up to you to guide the Vikings to victory. We'll show you where to strike once your blade is hot!

NIFLBERG

BRIGHTHELM SETTLEMENT

REQUIREMENTS:	Talk to the Shaman, talk to the Chieftain
OPTIONAL GOALS:	Talk to all civilians, hunt for gold, search the nearby beach, free several Vikings
ENEMIES PRESENT:	None

Freya returns Skarin to Brighthelm, his strength, weapons, and armor intact. He's ready to fight, but he must speak to several people before rushing into the wilderness. People who have something important to say have icons over their heads. Approach these individuals and find out what they know about your situation and the state of the war.

Look around the area where you begin. Skarin starts near the Brighthelm Leystone. You will return to this area often; it's the closest Leystone to all of the stores you need in Niflberg. The blacksmith is here to give Skarin elemental runes; the general store is here for healing potions, maps, and throwing axes; and you can make money by bringing Mead back to the village.

All in all, there is plenty to do, and you should wander around to find the gold that people have made available to the warriors of Brighthelm. There are bags of gold throughout the village, and there are several more lucrative urns to break as well. Don't be shy about taking all of this money; it's there for you, and the people of Brighthelm know that it will be put to a good cause.

Gold Abounds

You probably won't find all of the gold in Brighthelm during your first pass. Use the money you find during the first forays into the wilderness to purchase the maps for gold bags, urns, and treasure chests. These are invaluable for making even more money in the future. The sooner you buy them the more they pay for themselves!

Shaman Asta stands on the road, just below the Leystone area. Talk to her before going too far into the village. She explains some of what has happened to you, though she is somewhat unhinged. Being touched by the spirits doesn't make people terribly coherent!

Shopkeeper Osgood owns the general store, and he is on the village's western side. You can't talk to him yet; his store doesn't have any stock. All of the problems at Hilltop Farm have caused supplies to run dry here in Brighthelm, so you can't purchase any goodies until that situation is resolved.

The blacksmith is down at the base of the hill. You can find several hundred gold in Brighthelm, so it's entirely possible to buy your first elemental rune before you start to explore Niflberg. Fire and Ice are both very good choices here. Fire is more offensive, and it leads to faster military victories. Ice is more defensive, and helps to keep Skarin and his allies alive. You should even consider buying the first level of both!

Chieftain Haral is down by the gates of Brighthelm. He won't open the way into Niflberg until he talks with you. The Chieftain is extremely pleased that Skarin has survived the rigors of combat, regardless of how strange his reappearance may be. But things are not well in Brighthelm and throughout Niflberg. Many warriors have fallen, and still more are captured through the region. You must find these Vikings, save them, and boost your army's strength before taking on the Legion at the Gorge. Once that is done, you can start to retake northern Niflberg and eventually siege Darkwater, the local capital.

ODDASTRONG, THE LONG BEACH

REQUIREMENTS:	None
OPTIONAL GOALS:	Get two kegs of Niflberg Mead, free six Vikings
ENEMIES PRESENT:	None

Many small bags of gold are spread around the beach north of Brighthelm. Currently, no enemies attack the town from that direction, so Skarin can explore without risking himself. Take the gold that you find and look for surviving Vikings to free. Most of the warriors out there were lashed to poles and left to die a foul death, exposed to the elements. It's too late to help those poor kin. You can just hope that their valor was enough to send them to Valhalla and that these ignominious deaths will not rob Freya of even more good men.

The beached longships are of no use for now. They are interesting to look at, but there are too many local problems to even think about sailing away. This is no time for honorable raiding!

One cluster of living Vikings is on the beach's western side. Free them by approaching the stake to which they are lashed, and tap the controller button quickly to untie the men. These are the first new warriors to join your army. Before you go too far from there, scout around for some Niflberg Mead. Those barrels are worth a huge sum of gold back in Brighthelm; just talk to the beermaster.

A second keg of Mead is on the beach's eastern side, in a narrow section of sand that is probably underwater at high tide. Look at the end of that spot to see three more Vikings that need your help. It's a good thing that you were diligent, else those hapless men would have drown before long.

DON'T WALK OFF THE DEEP END

Niflberg Mead acquired

Skarin is wearing too much heavy armor and equipment for a long swim. He can step into the shallow end of the beaches and rivers throughout Midgard, but he dies quickly if you lead him in over his head. For the same reason, you must be extremely careful of jumping over cliff edges. Landing in deep water is a death sentence for Skarin.

HILLTOP FARM

REQUIREMENTS:	Kill the defending grunts, free the Viking captives, talk to Miller Tait when you are done
OPTIONAL GOALS:	Search the treasure chest by the windmill
ENEMIES PRESENT:	A moderate number of Grunts

After saving the six men on the beach, return to Brighthelm and use the eastern gate to leave town. Turn north, off the road, and look on your map. Hilltop Farm is clearly marked, and in game you can use the map to mark the farm as your current target. This leaves the spot up on your Brisingamen and makes it much easier to find your way there.

Your first fight against the Legion comes almost as soon as you leave the safe region around Brighthelm. A lone grunt patrols the road, looking for signs of Viking activity. He runs over to Skarin, blade drawn and looking for death. Use the block command and notice how easy it is to ward off a sole grunt. Just keep facing the fiend, and he can never hurt you. Then, when you have learned this lesson well, punish your opponent with a series of fast attacks. Three or four of these rips apart the grunt. When the slow attack icon appears, press the corresponding button and score your first finishing move! The fatalities look wicked, and you receive far more elemental orbs than if you just beat the grunt to death.

Follow the winding area that leads up the hills toward the farm. There are a few gold bags left out in the wilderness, though they may still be hard to spot without your treasure maps. Not many grunts guard the way, so you probably have only one more warm-up encounter before reaching the top.

You have a choice when making your assault in Hilltop Farm. The fast route is to rush up the southern hill. This saves about a minute in circling the hill and coming up the northern road. The fast route is convenient, but it doesn't easily give you a surprise attack. Many of the enemies are located on the farm's southern end and will spot Skarin's approach.

Taking the long way gives you more cover and allows Skarin to face a few of the enemies in seclusion, thinning the group's overall numbers before a chaotic a battle ensues.

There is a third option, which, in some ways, gives you the best of both worlds. Follow the southern route up the hill for a fast entry to the farm, but stay at long range and keep your distance from the buildings at first. Skirt the farm and enter on the eastern side, where there are some sheds and bales of hay. Fight the few grunts there, and you end with a smoother flow of combat without having to approach slowly!

Either way, Freya tells you about the farm as you enter its perimeter. She continues to do this for most of the areas that Skarin visits. Some of the information she gives you is downright useful. Other messages are interesting but don't shed light on your tactical concerns. In this case, she simply explains the history of Hilltop Farm and the necessity of retaking it.

The fighting itself isn't so tough. There are a handful of grunts, and the fight is quite manageable whether you are playing on Normal or Hard difficulty. Block while you lure the targets toward you, and then quickly punish attackers with two or three fast attacks. Use longer combos when there aren't many enemies nearby. When there are larger groups, use only single or double hits to avoid taking much damage from peripheral targets.

Once you slay all of the grunts, you must free the Vikings in the large cage. Approach the wooden structure and tap the "interact" button quickly to rip apart the beams that secure it. Vikings spill out and quickly arm themselves, ready to finish off any grunts that you've missed, though usually there aren't many left.

If you purchased one of the elemental runes before leaving Brighthelm, use your power now to buff these Vikings and see how the effect works. It's a quick process: just hold down the button for elemental magic and press a second button to select which elemental type to use. There is an achievement for buffing a large number of Vikings later in the game, so it's always nice to get big groups like this one.

Don't leave Hilltop Farm even after the area is secure. Look for Miller Tait. He comes out of the main building and has an icon over his head to show that he needs to speak to you. He tells you about the Lost Cargo that is nearby, which is necessary to get the general store up and running. He also lends you his support, giving strong words to show that he and his people believe in what you are doing.

Search the area near the windmill, on the western side of Hilltop Farm. There is a chest of gold there, and you need all the money you can get this early on in the war.

RETRIEVING THE LOST CARGO

REQUIREMENTS:	Open the treasure chest and return its contents to Shopkeeper Osgood in Brighthelm
OPTIONAL GOALS:	None
ENEMIES PRESENT:	A few Grunts

Make sure Skarin heals from his encounter at the farm. Outside of combat, he returns to perfect health quickly. Just watch the health bar climb, and notice that it fills even faster when Skarin isn't doing anything. Hold still and watch the farm settle back into its routine. Then hurry off on your next quest when Skarin is good to go!

The Lost Cargo is very close to Hilltop Farm. Run down the hill and destroy the few grunts that are close to the cart. Look on your map if you have trouble seeing the cargo—it's also marked as Map Point 2 on the map provided with this walkthrough.

There are only a few defenders at the site of the Lost Cargo, and they can't really stop Skarin. Start building up your elemental magic bar again, and then loot the chest when the area is clear. Bring the goods back to Shopkeeper Osgood. He then opens the general store in Brighthelm. Use the money you've already amassed to purchase either the health rune or some of the treasure maps. Both have major benefits. The health improvement is permanent, so it helps Skarin for the rest of the game! The treasure maps help you find all of the out-of-the-way treasure.

When you're strapped for cash, it's usually best to buy only the treasure map for the gold bags. These are the hardest treasure items to notice visually, and their map is the least expensive one to buy!

THE ANCIENT RUINS

REQUIREMENTS:	Free the Viking prisoners, discover part of the Dragon Amulet
OPTIONAL GOALS:	Collect more money and visit the Arena afterward
ENEMIES PRESENT:	Grunts

You still don't have enough allies to siege the bridge that leads into northern Niflberg. Hel has well over a hundred troops protecting the gap, and a champion leads them. Even the best warriors in the world couldn't face all of that alone.

So, hit the Ancient Ruins first and see if there are more Vikings there. After you purchase any supplies that you can afford, leave Brighthelm again and turn south after exploring the area along the road.

A Dark Nook

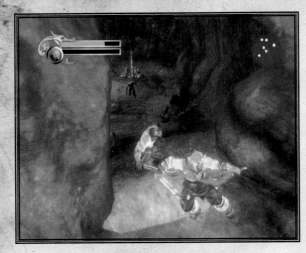

There is a small cave on the northern side of the ruins (marked as Map Point 3). It's somewhat easy to miss, so keep an eye on the side of the path. Several Vikings are trapped inside, and a few armed grunts guard them.

Stay at the lip of the cave to prevent Skarin from being flanked. Use fast attacks and blocking to punish the captors without risking yourself.

When the work is done, save the Viking inside. This is a good deed, and it helps you in your upcoming battle; all of the people you've freed aid you in the attack, and every man counts!

Beyond that, there are several bags of gold inside the cave. It's always nice to get paid for your fighting, so look carefully and loot everything in sight before you leave.

There is a Leystone on the eastern side of the Ancient Ruins. You need to visit these Leystones only one time to activate them. Afterward, Skarin can jump with impunity between Leystones he's visited. This particular Leystone is so far to the south that it isn't as tactically useful as some other Leystones, but it gets you close to the Arena. That is a very good thing, because Skarin must visit the Arena often to learn all of his special moves!

It's time to free your friends! Follow the small strip of ruins along the southern cliff. This passes the Leystone and a strange dragon altar. You find only a couple of grunts down there, so this route avoids a huge fight. There is also a convenient urn to grab along the way, and you're probably starving for wealth now. Take the money and continue.

Draw the last guard you see away from the cage of Vikings that he guards. Fight this grunt in the south so that none of Hel's people realize what is happening. Then break open the cage and use your elemental magic to buff the Vikings inside. They rush the remaining cluster of grunts, and you can enjoy a fast and easy slaughter! It doesn't get any better than that—well, actually it does, because there is an even bigger fight coming up soon. Still, that rush is beautiful when you perform it perfectly.

Jump across the broken bridge and use the southern road that leads into the ruins. Alternatively, you can avoid the bridge, run all the way to the east, and then come into the Ancient Ruins from the Arena side. Both options get you to the same place without a great deal of fighting, so it's more a matter of preference. If you wish to grab a special move or two right now, take the eastern route first. Look on your map, mark the Arena, and stop there before climbing back up the cliff. Get Thor's Hammer some time soon; that is arguably the most powerful of the inexpensive moves that Skarin can learn.

Additionally, there is a keg of Niflberg Mead on the beach, not far from the Dueling Arena. Look along the edge of the cliff for this, along with an urn that you can break and loot.

If you bring Skarin in from the north or down the main path into the Ruins, it is *much* harder to win. You have to fight off the entire cluster of grunts without any backup. They hound and harass Skarin, and it's a long fight in which you are forced to give ground, pick off grunts one at a time, and sometimes even run away to heal. This takes quite a while because you must get out of combat for Skarin to heal.

After all of the grunts in the area are killed, talk to Warrior Cadby. He tells you about Havelock, a Viking who was with the others during their ambush. Cadby says that Havelock was acting strangely, and now nobody knows where he is. It sounds like you should look around for Havelock and see what really happened during the ambush. This conversation causes a new mark to appear on your map, on the eastern shoreline. That is your next quest!

Before you leave the Ancient Ruins, walk to the northern side of the area and search for a treasure chest. That gets you a nice sum of gold, but there is even more important treasure above. Skarin can climb onto a broken section of wall very close to the chest. This leads onto a ledge that is easy to traverse as long as you are careful. Leap from that area to another tiny ledge, and sidestep over to the left.

Jump over to keep moving along the set of ledges, and hop up to a higher tier at the end of the path. The walkways wrap around the Ruins from there, but they dead-end at a wall with a great deal of overgrowth. Push Skarin into the wall and watch as he grabs hold of the vines. Climb left and down until you can get below another ledge, and then slip up onto it. It's then a simple run to reach another chest. This one has the Dragon Gem known as Hugin. You'll absolutely need this before long.

Retrace your path, hop down to the lower ledges, and then drop from there to the floor of the area. Collect any final gold you wish and move on.

WHAT HAPPENED TO HAVELOCK?

REQUIREMENTS:	Find Havelock and do what needs to be done
OPTIONAL GOALS:	Get another keg of Niflberg Mead and visit the Arena again, as necessary
ENEMIES PRESENT:	Grunts and Archers

There is Niflberg Mead on the eastern beach. You can pick this up while you walk from the Ancient Ruins up to Havelock's location on the map.

There is a beached longship near Havelock's position, and there are Legion grunts all over the place. Havelock is up there with them, but it doesn't look like he is a prisoner—a grim piece of news. He talks to Skarin briefly, and then it's a fight for survival.

Back away to deal with the early trio of grunts that attacks. Use the beached ship to block enemy sightlines and to avoid the arrows fired from archers in the distance.

Next, rush to the wooden planks and hop up to fight the archers. You can do this without attracting Havelock's attention or his two remaining grunts—just stay to the left as you move forward. Cut through the undefended archers and then leap down to slay the grunts. Do this quickly, and you can fight Havelock one-on-one. His sword attacks are easy to block, and you should respond with fast attacks. Havelock has no chance.

Take the traitor's Helmet and return that to Cadby at the Ancient Ruins. Cadby hears your news, responds appropriately, and tells you to talk to Torv. Torv is the innkeeper back in Brighthelm, and he's the one who needs the Niflberg Mead; he stands near the drinking area, at the foot of Brighthelm's hill. You can now turn in the casks you've collected. They are worth a good sum of gold. Use the nearby Leystone to reach Brighthelm quickly, and purchase any treats you want. Then look on your map to find your next target.

RETRIEVING YOUR BIRTHRIGHT

REQUIREMENTS:	Slay a Legion Champion and take his Battlehorn
OPTIONAL GOALS:	Grab the Hilltop Farm Leystone
ENEMIES PRESENT:	Grunts and a Champion

Feel free to walk all the way up to the area marked as "Battle Horn" on your map (Map Point 7 on this walkthrough's map). It's a shorter trip to use the Ruins Leystone, but you might want to take the overland route for monetary reasons. By now, you probably have one or more of the treasure maps from Osgood's store. That makes it easier to find loot out in the wild, and you can stop by Hilltop Farm to see if you missed anything there.

This is also a good time to get the Hilltop Farm Leystone if you haven't found it already. Look at Map Point 6 and search there until you see the small pillar of stone. This Leystone is rather valuable because it gets you so close to the Gorge area. The next two quests are somewhat difficult when you first get acquainted with them, so it's comforting to know that you can leap right back into the action if Skarin gets torn up.

The champion with your Battle Horn patrols the road close to the Gorge. He has a handful of grunts to help defend the region, but they aren't nearly the threat that he is. Champions endure a huge amount of damage, and they require a lot of dodging from Skarin. Keep the fight as safe as possible by killing off the grunts quickly. Use a throwing axe or two to hit the first few at range, and turn your attention to slaying the others while you avoid the champion.

LET GRAVITY DO YOUR WORK

You can certainly defeat this champion through honorable combat, and we'll tell you how to do that. But it's nice to have options. If the battle goes poorly, you can eliminate the champion without much fuss.

Lure the big guy over to the cliff's edge and slip around to his flank. Follow that with your block attack (hold the block button and make fast attacks). Essentially, these blows are body checks. They don't inflict much damage, but they knock targets backward, away from Skarin. You'll get a laugh when the champion goes over the cliff's edge!

Once the champion is alone, you can fight with much more comfort. Most of the big guy's attacks are obvious, though they are still dangerous. He pulls back and makes either a single swing or a series of wide attacks. Use your dodge to avoid the initial swing, and come forward only to punish the champion after you see him lose his momentum. Hit the fiend with a few fast attacks, and end with one of your special moves.

Repeat this a few times and wait for the champion to lean over, weary and exposed. The first button to press appears as an icon over his head—you must press it to begin the finishing moves. Watch the buttons carefully and tap them as best you can. Any failure forces you to repeat part of the fight against the champion, so be careful!

Purchase a Meal from Brighthelm if you need any assistance in this encounter. The temporary boost to Skarin's health makes a huge difference in fights like this one, and spending such a trivial sum of gold isn't a big deal.

Skarin collects the Skirmish Key and the Battle Horn when the champion dies. These are the final implements he needs before fighting the Battle of Slaterdale. Finish any last errands in town, be sure that you've bought at least one of the elemental runes, and go into your map. Highlight the Gorge area and "Initiate Your Attack" to start the fight.

The Army Comes at Your Behest

You can initiate these battles as soon as all of the qualifying conditions are met. You can't fight the Gorge battle until you liberate all of the Viking clans in the area and acquire the Battle Horn. Future battles have more requirements, but the tasks you must complete are usually spelled out quite clearly.

Once you prepare the army, they attack the location whenever you tell them to. In other words, you *do not* have to take Skarin to the Gorge to initiate the fight. He can be in Brighthelm, sunning himself at the beach, or busy ripping the arms off of evil grunts. Just use the map and watch the fun start.

THE BATTLE OF SLATERDALE

Fighting for Control of the Gorge

Size of Battle:	Skirmish
Number of Stages:	One
Enemies Involved:	Many Grunts and Archers, a few Warriors
Can You Use Dragons:	No

Slaterdale is the site for this skirmish. It's not nearly as difficult or complex as some of the upcoming battles, and it serves as ideal training for commanding the army. Several dozen Viking men are ready to fight at your side, and even more grunts and archers are aligned against them. Show Hel's Legion that their fate is sealed!

The encounter's initial moments are intense. Your army marches up toward the gates of the Gorge when a wave of grunts races out to begin the melee. If you have elemental magic accrued already, use Fire or Ice to improve your allies' abilities. This makes the fight much easier for them.

Use finishing moves against every enemy that gets in your way. This allows Skarin to pull in much more elemental energy, keeping his troops at their best. It also reduces casualties for allied Vikings and looks exciting.

After you pass through the gate, there are six Vikings to untie on the area's right side. Should you choose, you can get these men after the battle, or you can take a moment to save them after your clear the archers.

A treasure chest is not far from the Viking prisoners, and various bags of loot litter the ground. You should probably wait until after the fight to play treasure hunter, but it's fun to snag an odd bag or two as you slice through grunts.

Once you beat the mass of grunts inside the gates, a second stage of fighting commences. More Legion troops pour into the area and attack your army's flanks. The fighting becomes more chaotic, forcing you to watch your back more often. However, this presents even more opportunities to hit Legion troops when they aren't expecting it. Use the area's hills and drops to avoid fighting clusters of enemies as they arrive. Get above them and drop down on their rear, dealing heavy damage while the foes are busy with rank-and-file Vikings.

The remainder of the battle is a slugfest. You don't encounter any enemies that you've never seen before, and your warriors have a substantial edge—they are tougher, and Hel's troops don't have any shamans to summon reinforcements. You shouldn't have any big problems.

THE ENCAMPMENT ABOVE THE GORGE

REQUIREMENTS:	Kill all Legion troops in the area
OPTIONAL GOALS:	Save the trio of Vikings up there and the trio of Vikings down in the lower cave
ENEMIES PRESENT:	Grunts and a Warrior

Search for loot and for additional allies after your battle is over. Climb the small path above the Gorge and look for the Legion Encampment there. Three Vikings are tied up in the middle of the camp, and half a dozen of Hel's troops are watching them. Focus on the grunts early in the fight, and use burst damage with slow rage attacks to kill them as they arrive. This prevents Skarin from getting outflanked.

After you kill all of the enemies and save the Vikings, look for gold in the area. There are quite a few bags lying around, and who else is going to use the money?

Finally, there is a small cave in the Gorge area's southern region. It is tucked away at the end of the path, and you might miss it if you aren't thorough. Just folow the small dirt path all the way south, and don't hop down onto the normal road. Turn left with the path and look for the cave. There are three grunts inside and a fair amount of treasure, and you can save three more Vikings after a short fight.

CROSSING THE GORGE

REQUIREMENTS:	Find the locked cave in the Gorge area and cross into northern Niflberg
OPTIONAL GOALS:	None
ENEMIES PRESENT:	Grunts, Archers, Warriors, and an Assassin

Unfortunately, Hel's commanders in Niflberg are reasonably intelligent. They knew that the Gorge forces weren't reinforced enough to withstand a major assault. And that is why they've sealed off the continent's northern section from the far side of the cliffs. Your victory in Slaterdale was extremely important, but the Vikings can't cross the bridge yet. Someone has to slip around to the region's far side and raise the bridge manually. It won't be easy, and Skarin is the only Viking who can dependably make the attempt.

Look for the locked cave on the eastern side of the Gorge. It isn't far from where most of the battle took place. Break open the huge lock by rapidly pressing the interaction button, and wander through the small corridor beyond. There is a modest amount of gold to loot, and it's all easy to see. But be wary as you walk; there are a several archers and grunts along this route.

The caverns aren't large at all, so you should get through them within a few moments. The other side has more fighting on a grassy ledge that winds around the mountains. Follow this to reach a small, wooden bridge. This is the backup route for anyone who wants to reach northern Niflberg. Archers continually fire down on Skarin as he tries to cross the bridge. Keep moving to avoid these attacks without any major trouble.

Climb the northern cliffs when you arrive, and slice through the archers in vengeance for their cheap tactics. Have a bit of fun with them if you like by shoulder-barging them off the cliff's edge. It's always amusing when Hel's goons plummet to their watery graves from of such a low-damage attack.

You find a bridge at the top of the path. Use this to leap across the gap in the trail. If you mess up the jump and fall, simply retrace your steps and try again. There aren't any penalties for falling, and there are two small bags of gold in the depression anyway. Collect them and kill the measly grunt that guards them before you proceed.

Hop onto the rocky ledges and climb in that direction. Deal with two more grunts during the climb. They are alone and offer little resistance, and you claim a suitable reward when you reach the top of the next section: there's a Leystone there! Now you won't have to worry if you make a mistake and tumble off the cliffs.

This Leystone is especially comforting when you look over the next bridge. A warrior guards it, and two archers on the far side can cover him. This seems like a tactically challenging situation, but there are ways to make it easier. You can just charge the warrior and push him back as you fight. This prevents the arrows from being a major threat.

Alternatively, you can be extremely brave and try to kill the warrior outright. Do this by blocking as you sidestep around the warrior. This places Skarin's back to the edge of the bridge. One slip and you'll lose instantly. However, the same is true for the warrior. If you block his attack, sidestep quickly, and then check him, the fight will be over before it really starts.

The safest option is to make a fighting retreat. Hit the warrior and step back to avoid the arrows. Block his reprisal, and repeat the process. It's slow, but you will suffer very little damage.

Obliterate the archers when you are done. They are trivial without their warrior to protect them!

A single grunt hides behind a tree not much farther ahead. Don't let him ambush you! Turn the tide by coming around the corner defensively. Block the grunt and toss him over the edge. He should realize about halfway down that Skarin was the wrong Viking to mess with.

Hop over the small gap in the trail and get ready for a more serious fight. Three grunts and two warriors protect a nearby cave. Lure the grunts down to your position and fight them there. Afterward, retreat and rest so that Skarin has all of his health when he engages the two warriors. The heavier enemies aren't too bad, but you still haven't fought many before, so it's better to err on the side of caution.

You won't have an easy time getting to the warriors' backs. It's easier to toss an axe into one warrior, inflicting some damage and distracting him. Rush the other and wail on the fiend with fast attacks and a mix of slow rage attacks for extra damage. By the time the first warrior is ready to come after you, his buddy should be nearly dead.

The fight eases considerably with one foe down, because lone warriors can't hit Skarin very well. Stay in a defensive position, wait for the warrior to waste his attacks, and then counterattack with ferocity.

Enter the warriors' cave and pick up the small bags of gold and the urn along the main tunnel. The grunts inside aren't aware of your presence, so you have the option to ambush them with throwing axes, stealth attacks (if you purchased Fenrir's Bite), or a charged slow attack.

The cave's inner portion has two tiers. Skarin starts on the upper tier. There's a ledge around the outside of the level. It isn't well guarded, so the main challenge is to make the jump at the walkway's end. It's safe to drop down to the lower tier between the ledge and a far platform..

Steal the chest from the bottom and rest for a moment. There's an assassin ahead, and you haven't fought any of them yet. These enemies deliver quite a bit of damage if you aren't ready for them. Don't turn your back on them! They leap onto their victims and rip into them for as long as they can. If this happens, shake your movement stick back and forth to throw off the assassin.

Use a strong offense to defeat these quick targets. Fast rage attacks and short combos work wonderfully. Assassins can hurt Skarin badly, but they can't take what they dish out. Slice through this assassin early in the fight, and he has little chance to return the favor.

CLEARING THE ENCAMPMENT

REQUIREMENTS:	Free the Vikings nearby
OPTIONAL GOALS:	Assassinate a Horn Blower
ENEMIES PRESENT:	Grunts (one has a Battle Horn)

There are a few things to do in the east before you continue your journey. Skarin has broken through the cave and can move back through the area whenever he wants, but the fields outside the cave are still rife with enemy troops.

A grunt with a battle horn is not far from the cave's exit. This is a good opportunity to kill an enemy with a throwing axe. He dies from a single toss, so you don't have to spend much money replacing the axe. Stealth attacks also work well if you lack axes. Should you be out of luck on both counts, the best method is to charge a slow attack and unleash its full fury on the horn blower.

SO WHAT HAPPENS IF HE BLOWS THE HORN?

You don't lose automatically if a horn blower manages to call his allies. However, horn sounds can carry across large distances. Grunts run from far and wide to get in on the Viking-killing goodness, and you might be better off retreating if the press of enemies looks too hard to handle.

There aren't enough grunts in one place to make the fight dangerous as long as you assassinate the horn blower. Kill the few defenders near the cage on the valley's right side, and free your Viking allies. They mop up the rest of the opposition and are ready to assist you later, during the siege on Darkwater.

Travel west, away from the encampment. There is another Leystone there, and it's important for you to get it right now. Seizing this Leystone effectively eliminates the travel time and hassle of getting between northern and southern Niflberg. Even if you don't open the drawbridge right now, Skarin can hop wherever he needs to go just by going to a Leystone!

Look on the western side of the outpost to find the real way into the building. Leap over the broken section of wall to get into the courtyard. Three more grunts attack you there, but you have plenty of room to maneuver. Just don't stay near the initial wall; a pesky archer from above tries to hit you if you stay out in the open.

THE BRIDGE ISN'T TOO FAR

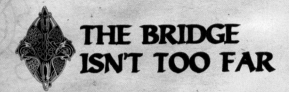

REQUIREMENTS:	Raise the Drawbridge and give your army access to northern Niflberg
OPTIONAL GOALS:	Loot the place
ENEMIES PRESENT:	Grunts

Observe the drawbridge from the cliffs above the outpost. Grunts patrol below, and what you see is only the tip of the iceberg. There are more grunts inside the outpost, so this isn't a place to take lightly.

Jumping down from the cliffs inflicts some damage, so it's better to come from the north if you're worried about the fighting afterward. Take out the grunts outside the buildings first. Let them come over to you, and dispatch them safely. Or hurl axes at their backs for sneakier killing.

Use the doorjambs to limit how much the enemies inside the outpost can rush you. There are three in the eastern room, which doesn't actually lead anywhere. Kill one from the doorway, and then use combos to take out the next two in relative safety.

FOR YOUR HEALTH

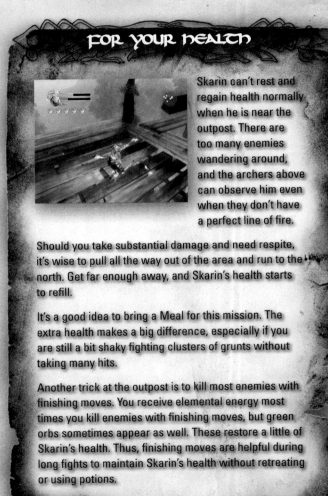

Skarin can't rest and regain health normally when he is near the outpost. There are too many enemies wandering around, and the archers above can observe him even when they don't have a perfect line of fire.

Should you take substantial damage and need respite, it's wise to pull all the way out of the area and run to the north. Get far enough away, and Skarin's health starts to refill.

It's a good idea to bring a Meal for this mission. The extra health makes a big difference, especially if you are still a bit shaky fighting clusters of grunts without taking many hits.

Another trick at the outpost is to kill most enemies with finishing moves. You receive elemental energy most times you kill enemies with finishing moves, but green orbs sometimes appear as well. These restore a little of Skarin's health. Thus, finishing moves are helpful during long fights to maintain Skarin's health without retreating or using potions.

The next step is to climb the vines onto the outpost's higher level, but steal the urn from the courtyard and the chest from inside the room around the corner. The gold from these adds up quickly! There are two more grunts inside the room with the chest. Run in quickly and assault the first grunt with a long combo. The second grunt is resting and doesn't get up in time to help.

Look for the overgrown sections of wall to spot the vines that Skarin can climb. There are two archers on the roof, and they get quite upset when they realize that Skarin is jumping up next to them. Clean up those foes and cross to the other side of the roof. Drop down through the hole there, get some treasure, and drop yet another level. You have to beat two warriors in that room, but you've survived similar tasks before. You can do it again now!

Use the cramped quarters to prevent the warriors from gaining an easy approach to you. Stay against one of the walls, and wail on the first warrior to possibly push him out into the room. Even if he doesn't budge, you can stick him with fast rage attacks or short combos. As soon as his shield breaks, you should crush him with a slow rage attack. The second warrior is meat once his buddy dies.

Use the crank in that room to lower the drawbridge. You've done it! Northern Niflberg is now vulnerable to Viking attack, and you need only to build your forces before Darkwater is yours. Well, you also have to find a dragon willing to help with the siege, but that should be a piece of cake, right?

EXPLORING THE SHIPWRECK

REQUIREMENTS: Kill the Legion Grunts and steal the Medical Supplies
OPTIONAL GOALS: Save a trio of Vikings
ENEMIES PRESENT: Grunts

There is a shipwreck along the southern side of the coast. Three Vikings were seized there and are tied up west of the wreck. A cluster of grunts enjoys a comfy fire closer to the area. Before you proceed to the Quarry, head over to this spot and ambush the grunts. Use an axe or stealth attack to remove the first defender, and then plow into the middle of the remaining three.

The chest next to this lot has a set of Medical Supplies. They'll certainly come in handy, especially with so many Vikings involved in the war. Afterward, head west along the beach and free the prisoners to gain three more allies in the upcoming fight!

DOWN INTO THE QUARRY

REQUIREMENTS: Free the Quarry workers and kill all Legion forces
OPTIONAL GOALS: Get wealthy from the multitude of gold items
                      around the Quarry
ENEMIES PRESENT: Grunts, Archers, and Warriors

The Quarry is one of the few sites that has almost as much defense as a town. There are archers and grunts everywhere, and warriors support them in a few spots. Skarin has a lot on his hands if he wants to clear the entire area by himself, but there are tricks to make this battle much easier.

First, quite a few Quarry workers are held captive in the Quarry's northern area. You can free them before all the defenders are dead, and the Vikings will be overjoyed to help you with the remaining Legion troops.

Don't try to leap down into the Quarry from one of the higher tiers. You need your health to complete this quest, and a big fall won't improve the situation. Come around from the western side and fight along the upper ledge's length. This winds its way down into the Quarry, and the wooden railings around the sides prevent archers from giving you trouble.

The heavier fighting starts when you reach the bottom. Archers in the distance and on a walkway above try to hassle Skarin as grunts advance on him. Use long chains of fast attacks to wade through troops and give the archers a moving target. Look for a ramp on the left side that leads to the archers' ledge. Clear out those goons and notice the chest they were guarding; it contains only money, but you should definitely come back for it later.

Once the archers are down, you are mostly clear to save the Quarry workers. Just kill the guards that are close to their enclosure, and use the elemental energy you've gathered during the attack to buff the workers on their way out. They have no trouble defeating the rest of the Legion.

Search the Quarry thoroughly. There are hundreds of gold coins lying around, and you are probably working on some of the more expensive special moves at this point. They cost a fair sum, and every bag counts!

When you are ready to leave, talk to Quarry Master Kell, in the middle of the depression. Kell is willing to lend his people to the cause, but first he needs some help eliminating an elite patrol to the north. Bring up your map and initiate the attack at your leisure.

The men from the Quarry set up a very good ambush, and they attack the grunts from two sides. Archer support is in your favor, and the enemies won't know how to react properly. Everything soon devolves into a frantic melee, but your team has the advantage!

Use elemental magic as soon as you can. Lightning and Fire both work very well, as this is *not* a defensive encounter. Thor's Hammer is a wonderful special move to rely on during the fight. This attack kills the grunts quickly and avoids many peripheral attacks as Skarin hops from victim to victim.

LOOK WHERE YOU'RE GOING

Don't go into the area where the elite patrol wanders until the Quarry workers have helped you destroy this group. Skarin can't kill all of these enemies by himself, and they are very aggressive in rushing after him. It's not easy to get away once the whole group is after you, so exercise extreme caution and avoid using the roads north of the Quarry.

Make sure that all grunts are dead, and the battle soon ends. Watch the brief scene and wander west briefly to search for the Quarry Leystone. Make sure you find this (Map Point 16) and then return to the Quarry. Master Kell honors his agreement. Only a few targets remain before your assault on Darkwater can begin!

AMBUSHING THE ELITE PATROL

REQUIREMENTS:	Destroy the Legion patrol
OPTIONAL GOALS:	None
ENEMIES PRESENT:	Grunts

THE MONASTERY CAVE

REQUIREMENTS:	Save the Vikings in the Monastery Cave
OPTIONAL GOALS:	Bring the Medical Supplies the first time you enter the cave
ENEMIES PRESENT:	Grunts and a Warrior

The Quarry Master gives you a set of explosives. These should do the trick for opening the Monastery Cave—there's a large gate with a lock at the caves' southern end. Interact with the gate to set the explosives, and make sure to be somewhere else in 20 seconds when they detonate.

The first tunnel doesn't stretch very far; it leads to an urn and a few grunts to kill. Use the side tunnel; to the right, when you want to continue. A beefy warrior guards that path, but he doesn't have any strong support.

You quickly reach a gap that you cannot cross with a normal jump. Climb to the bottom if you want a small bag of gold, and then use the ledge on the upper left side to sidestep across.

Warrior Ingemar and his troops are on the other side. The bad news is that Ingemar's people have been treated horribly, and many of them are either sick or injured, or both. Luckily, you encountered the grunts at the Shipwreck and stolen their Medical Supplies. Use these to save Ingemar's people, securing even more troops in the process.

NOW FOR THE NORTHERN CAVE

REQUIREMENTS:	Save a few more Vikings
OPTIONAL GOALS:	None
ENEMIES PRESENT:	Three Grunts

Walk north from the Monastery Cave, staying on the eastern side of the mountains. There is a tiny cave in the area that is very easy to miss—you must secure it! Three grunts hold a group of Vikings there, and it doesn't take more than a minute to complete the whole assault. Ambush the first grunt with a stealth attack, and rampage through the enemy on his left. You can probably beat the whole cave without taking a single hit.

RESTORE PEACE TO THE MONASTERY

REQUIREMENTS:	Defeat the Shaman at the Monastery
OPTIONAL GOALS:	Save groups of Vikings in and around the Monastery
ENEMIES PRESENT:	Grunts, Archers, a Champion, a Berserker, and a Shaman

Walk west from the cave, and use the northern path to reach the Monastery. There are archers and grunts in moderate numbers along the path. Use stealth and hide behind the rocks to the right if you want to make these fights more manageable. This makes it easier to ambush and kill patrolling grunts without a struggle. Throwing enemies off the cliff using shoulder barges is also viable.

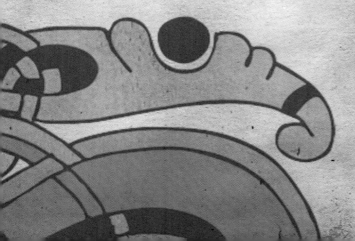

Either way, Skarin gets a chance to rest at the top of the cliff. Restore his health by waiting a moment, and then continue around the next bend. A grunt with a battle horn waits in the open. There are half a dozen troops with him, along with a few archers to assist. Either rush the horn blower or throw an axe or two at him to silence his musical ambitions. Then back away to kill the grunts that approach, simultaneously avoiding the archers' fire. Use the walls for cover, kill the grunts, and finish off the archers whenever you want.

Climb to the very top of the road and get the Monastery Leystone. This is a good one to have, because the fighting up here is intense and you won't have to run up the path again if you get hurt. There are also three Vikings to rescue near the top, though you must clear out a few enemies before saving them. A warrior, a few grunts, and an archer are spread along the road and the entrance.

There are quite a few grunts inside the main courtyard. You catch your first sight of the Monastery's leader—a shaman! These religious figures in Hel's Legion are known for their ability to summon the dead in great numbers. That explains why the Monastery is so well staffed with grunts.

Creep into the courtyard and ambush the first grunt and the horn blower beyond. This prevents Skarin from having to fight the whole courtyard at once. Instead, the grunts gradually notice him and trickle over, getting killed almost as quickly as they can arrive. If you fail to kill the horn blower, back away and fight the flood of grunts at the area's entrance.

MORE GRUNTS?

Skip

The glowing shaman summons pairs of grunts periodically until you chase him into the Monastery's upper levels. Just charge over to the shaman to chase away the coward. This gives you more freedom to clear the exiting grunts and save the nearby captives.

As a side note, you can kill grunts while the shaman summons them. They are vulnerable to all normal attacks, and they aren't fully aware of Skarin's presence at first. This leaves them susceptible to stealth moves as well!

Save the Vikings on the yard's right side when the grunts are dead. You can't help them until the area is clear because it takes too long to untie them; Skarin just gets stabbed in the back before he finishes.

A small room on the yard's left side has almost 100 gold. There are a few sleeping grunts in there. It's fun to ambush them and slap the trio around while you steal their goodies.

There is an open chamber with a berserker, two archers, and a grunt on the walkway's left side. Don't give the berserker time to approach. Rush the archers on your left; they are near a new Ley-stone. Charge them, push into their side room, and kill both archers as you build up your rage crystals. Next, use slow rage attacks to obliterate the berserker as soon as he is alone. Berserkers are easy to block when they are isolated, but they take a lot of damage to kill. That is why they are good to save for last when there are missile troops present.

Go into the room that the shaman was blocking before it ran off. Break the urn on the lower floor and then climb to the top. You soon spot the shaman again, at the walkway's far end. Run toward it and rip through the two grunts that are summoned. Hurrying lets you ambush one and fight the other in a very lopsided duel.

Use the small ledge around the corner to sidestep across a nasty gap. Leap the second break in the walkway, and don't freak out if you start to fall short—you should land on a stone outcropping. Pull yourself up if that happens, and cautiously proceed. Jump another broken area of the walkway and run across a line of planks.

The next turn in the passage is a trap. An assassin leaps from above and scurries onto Skarin's back. You can't avoid this, so the best tactic is to shake your movement stick quickly and throw off the fiend as soon as possible. Use fast attacks like Nidhogg's Strike (if you've learned it) to defeat the assassin before he can repeat his treacherous assault.

Loot all of the treasure in the Leystone room, and consider taking a trip back to Brighthelm. The crank in the next chamber opens the portcullis into another yard. Though the battle there is certainly winnable, it is the toughest encounter so far. Grabbing a few more throwing axes and a Meal would be a very good investment right now.

The fight itself has six grunts, two warriors, two archers, and a champion. Four of grunts come up to attack as soon as Skarin enters the room. Stay up top and fight them beyond archer range. Keep your back to the portcullis and knock a few of the grunts off the platform to give yourself a more manageable fight.

Use finishing moves against every single target in this encounter. You *need* the extra health that sometimes comes from these kills, and the spare elemental energy is also good. Save that energy for the fight on the lower level. Ice is the best element to use because it is very effective against all champions.

The other two grunts, the warriors, and the champion charge over once you come down. Before you engage them, free the six Vikings in the middle areas—there are three on each side. These men provide a distraction while you make your main attack.

Let the Vikings engage your enemies, and hop down to free the additional warriors tied up at the back of the yard. The warriors and the champion are usually quite distracted at this point. This leaves you free to kill the archers and grunts.

DON'T PLAY FAIR UNLESS YOU WANT TO

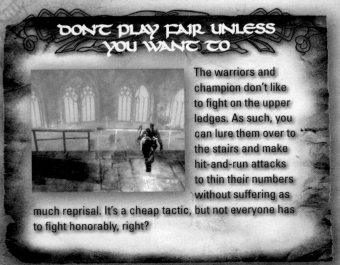

The warriors and champion don't like to fight on the upper ledges. As such, you can lure them over to the stairs and make hit-and-run attacks to thin their numbers without suffering as much reprisal. It's a cheap tactic, but not everyone has to fight honorably, right?

The double doors into the Monastery's deepest chamber are sealed, but all of the troops guarding them are now eradicated. Rest to full health and open the doors. Your last fight in the Monastery has arrived. The shaman is alone, save for the grunts that he can call forth from Hel's bosom. You can handle this!

Kill the initial two grunts. You can't ambush either of them this time, but they still aren't a huge threat. Destroy the five posts that surround the shaman next. You can't hurt the shaman directly while these shielding totems are in place. It takes only two fast attacks to destroy each totem.

Watch your back as you do this, because the shaman keeps summoning grunts. Fight the next two after you've brought down two or three totems. Then finish the rest of the targets after that pair dies. The shaman immediately becomes vulnerable. Use a finishing move to cut the monster in half.

This earns Skarin the Dragon Amulet. You now have both the Amulet itself and the Hugin Gem (from the Ancient Ruins). Together, these allow warriors to call upon the power of a local dragon, but there isn't enough power left in the Amulet to proceed.

Soon the way will be clear!

A QUICK WALK ON THE BEACH

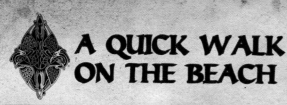

REQUIREMENTS:	Free another clan of Vikings
OPTIONAL GOALS:	Grab more loot
ENEMIES PRESENT:	A cluster of Grunts with a Horn Blower as their leader

Darkwater is marked clearly on your map, and you must infiltrate the infested city by yourself. It's a daunting proposition, but there are a few minor chores to do first. Run back to the eastern side of the map and go to Map Point 21 to get the Darkwater Leystone. That saves travel time in the future.

Next, continue east and look at Map Point 22 to find the last group of Vikings to liberate in Niflberg. There are a few grunts there with a horn blower, but there is no reason to be scared. There aren't enough enemies to worry you. Use slow rage attacks to plaster the grunts, and break your allies free as soon as the fighting ends.

Search the campsite for a treasure chest, and then run up the cliff path for even more gold. You can also find a keg of Niflberg Mead just beneath the cliffs, also to the east.

CHARGING THE AMULET

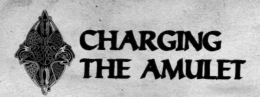

REQUIREMENTS:	Charge the Dragon Amulet
OPTIONAL GOALS:	Have fun and try not to be seen
ENEMIES PRESENT:	Too many to count or fight

Start at the Darkwater Leystone. Free the Vikings just west of the Leystone, and then slip north from there. This gets Skarin around the eastern side of the city. There are three Vikings tied to a post there, and they aren't far from your stealthy path inside Darkwater. Look at the walls and search for a banner hanging over the wall's edge. It's a foolish oversight by Hel's troops; anyone can climb over that and get into the city without being seen. Do so!

When you get inside, jump left over the small fence. Use stealth or one of your axes to kill the nearby grunt. Then wait for two patrolling troops to pass, oblivious to your presence. Stay near the east wall and kill another lone target by the southern corner. It's okay if you draw the attention of a few extra grunts here; it happens, and you can kill them in the corner without getting the whole city on your back.

Move west now, up onto the ramparts. Don't bother killing the archers there. They probably notice Skarin one way or the other, but speed is your ally. Charge past everyone and stay in the middle of the rampart. Otherwise, a stray arrow could knock you into the heavy packets of soldiers below.

Come down on the far side and ambush the single grunt waiting there with his back turned. Jump up the boxes beyond and kill another clueless grunt. Then charge the Dragon Amulet at the circle of stones that dominates the southwest portion of Darkwater. After that, jump over one of the nearby sections of wall and run away. You've done it!

SPEAKING WITH DRAGONS

REQUIREMENTS:	Take the charged Dragon Amulet to the Ancient Ruins
OPTIONAL GOALS:	Visit the Arena
ENEMIES PRESENT:	None

Use the Darkwater Leystone to travel back to the Ancient Ruins. Visit the Arena and buy any special moves that you don't have and can afford. This is one of the last times to access the Arena in Niflberg.

After that, walk back to the Leystone and keep going south around the edge of the cliffs. An old altar there was used in the past for communicating with dragons.

Pray at the altar and summon the young dragon Ari. You have done much to prove yourself, and this loyal creature joins the Viking cause. You have all the troops you need, and the assistance of a legendary dragon. Buy anything you want from Brighthelm now, because it's time to free Niflberg from Hel's tyranny!

THE BATTLE OF DARKWATER

FOR NIFLBERG!

Stage One

The two sides have come together in the field just south of Darkwater. Hel has committed the first wave of her grunts to the center of the field. A great champion who stands at the very front of their ranks leads them.

To the west is a single shaman, responsible for all reinforcements drawn into this stage of the battle. Many grunts, a berserker, and mystic shielding totems surround the shaman.

Charge the enemy troops in midfield, and kill their grunts with finishing moves as quickly as you can. Build up elemental energy, and then use ice to improve Skarin's weaponry. Attack the champion directly while influenced by ice and watch how quickly this leader dies. He drops two Dragon Runes. Use these immediately to blast the shaman and end the first wave!

Size of Battle:	Large
Number of Stages:	Three
Enemies Involved:	Countless Grunts, many Archers and Warriors, a few Berserkers, three Shamans, one Champion, and Hel's Harbinger
Can You Use Dragons:	Oh Yeah!

Stage Two

Hel's troops fall back into the city after you bloody their nose. They still receive reinforcements, because two more shamans are inside the gates. There are also more archers on the walls, able to support the grunts below.

Another champion is at the front of the enemy forces inside the gates. Get more elemental energy, and then repeat your ice assassination against this champion. Use his Dragon runes to kill the shaman on the right side; that one is deeper inside enemy territory and takes much more work to reach.

Turn left at the first junction, and advance with your soldiers until you see the only remaining shaman. Gutsy types can even run ahead of the army and attack the shaman's group without support. It's quite challenging, but practice and skilled use of rage attacks make it feasible.

Stage Three

The army is victorious once the second shaman falls, but the battle is not over for you! Skarin and Drakan, the champion of Hel's forces, must fight a duel. Drakan fights like a normal champion in some ways, but he's even tougher and has a few extra attacks.

First, Drakan delivers more damage. He can put down Skarin with only two or three hits if you aren't careful. You must dodge those big swings with great consistency, so don't go on full offense. Hit-and-run attacks are the way to win safely!

In the beginning, Drakan relies on his sword combos to hack at Skarin. Avoid these by making either two fast attacks or one slow rage attack on each run. Get in your shots and then press the block button and dodge as soon as Drakan pulls back his blade or ducks for a body check.

Later, Drakan throws a massive hook and chain to snare Skarin. Hit the mighty leader with Fafnir's Might to get him out of his routine. Or go fully defensive and sidestep before dodging to avoid the hook.

Be ready to press buttons quickly to finish the fight. There is a tiny window for the necessary button combination in the last moments. Failure restores a fair portion of Drakan's health. Tap the initial button to start the finishing move, and then press and hold the next button that pops up without delay.

Several scenes follow the duel's end, and Skarin has to leave Niflberg. There are other regions to save from Hel's influence, and little time remains.

GALCLIFF

the city of caldberg

north watchtower

farm

dragon stones

town of holdenfort

Landing camp

duel arena

ship's graveyard

ruins

coastal caves

still farm

south watch tower

quarry

galcliff

LANDING CAMP

REQUIREMENTS:	Talk to the Champion Jarl
OPTIONAL GOALS:	Purchase new upgrades from the general store and the blacksmith
ENEMIES PRESENT:	None

The epic continues on the southwestern side of Galcliff, where the landing party establishes itself and sets up shop. There are new runes to purchase from the blacksmith, and you have access to better throwing axes, new Meals, and greater health from the general store. If you have any money left over from your time in Niflberg, this is a good place to spend it.

Examine your map and get a feel for Galcliff. There are enemy positions to your east and to the south. Movement in this region is harder than in Niflberg. There are substantial mountains that block travelers on foot. This means you have to do some cave exploration soon.

Talk to Champion Jarl on the southeastern side of camp. He tells you about some of the local problems and urges you into action. Visit the Leystone to the east after you finish your conversation. Shaman Asta is there, and she tells you where the Dragon Stones are found in this region.

CAVE CAMP

REQUIREMENTS:	Free the prisoners
OPTIONAL GOALS:	Explore the Dragon Stones to the north
ENEMIES PRESENT:	Several Grunts and Archers led by two Warriors

There is a small camp of Viking prisoners to the southeast of the landing site. This is one of the first places that you should liberate in Galcliff. Explore the northern coast for a while, if you like, and climb up to the Dragon Stones. You can't interact with these yet, but they are poorly guarded by only a few archers and grunts. There is a little gold up there, and you can also spot the entrance to a very large cave complex farther east.

There is also a stake with three Vikings tied to it. Look to the road's northern side as you walk near the hilly region close to the landing site.

After you finish exploring, go to Map Point 3 and ambush the grunts on the camp's periphery. Stab any of the resting troops if you have time. Then hurry to kill off the archers before the rest of the camp has time to mobilize. Use rage attacks to kill the final grunts and warriors.

Free the prisoners in the wooden enclosure, and then talk to Warrior Hrut. Hrut urges you to assault the central cave and kill a great Legion champion that controls the area. He says that his people will aid you after the champion is dead. No problem; it's not like you to let a champion just wander around and do whatever he wants.

WEST CAMP

TURN UP THE HEAT AT THE DISTILLERY

REQUIREMENTS:	Free more Vikings
OPTIONAL GOALS:	None
ENEMIES PRESENT:	Very few Grunts, a Horn Blower, one Berserker, and a Warrior

REQUIREMENTS:	Seize the Distillery and make it operational again
OPTIONAL GOALS:	Visit the Distillery Leystone
ENEMIES PRESENT:	Many Grunts and Warriors

There's a motley group of Legion troops at the Western Camp, at Map Point 4. Their numbers are low, but they have some heavy hitters with them. The warrior of the group has a higher quality shield than some of those you've seen before. He can endure more hits from the front by a fair margin; level-two rage attacks are almost a necessity for bringing him down quickly. However, you can back over to the cliff's edge and knock him into the Viking camp. Let your buddies do the work for you, eh?

Stay on the northern side of the camp in general. The enemies come to you there. You can fight with plenty of room and still have the potential to knock enemies off if they become troublesome.

The tough grunt tries to hassle you while the other enemies pile on. Use a combo-ender to throw the tough grunt off of you. This buys time to defeat other targets without fear of getting ripped open. Freya's Chariot—two fast attacks and a slow attack as the combo-ender—is the best move for messing with tough grunts.

Free the Vikings from their cage once the enemies are dead. They don't demand anything from Skarin for their loyalty. They are simply glad to be alive!

Travel south toward the Distillery. The point is already marked on Skarin's map, though it's worth taking a detour along the western coast to pick up the Leystone at Map Point 5.

The Distillery is extremely well guarded. Hel doesn't want anyone to walk in and seize this place, because it could be very useful to the Vikings. The spirits that were previously made here aren't just good for having a fun time—they can be made into flame pots! The Legion is certainly flammable, and getting the stills operational would be quite nice.

There's an easy way and a hard way to take out the enemies here. Skarin can march in by the farm's northern end and lay waste to everything in his path. You must fight with great skill to defeat groups of grunts and warriors in close proximity. The early targets are easy to ambush and fight alone, but the enemies come in large numbers once a full alert is raised.

If you prefer a sneakier or more efficient route, creep toward the western side of the Distillery. There aren't many guards patrolling outside the fence there. Ambush these for silent kills, and then hop over the wall. Ambush or use throwing axes against guards near the prisoners' area, and then quickly slip around to free everyone. It's possible to accomplish all of this before the enemies really notice. You can then take the area with *many* Vikings at your side.

There is a small ambush after the Vikings retake the Distillery. A patrol wanders back into the compound, coming from the north. All of the Vikings hide, and presumably mop up the blood and guts from the first fight. Luckily, the Legion forces don't notice the damage and wander straight into the attack. Buff your allies against their foes, and enjoy the slaughter that erupts.

Talk to Distiller Njal when the area is again under Viking control. He clearly wants to help in the war effort, but he doesn't know all the tricks of the trade. His father was the real expert at making flame pots. The grim news is that his father was already killed by the Legion, but Njal believes that his father's old notes are intact. He marks a set of Ruins on your map and suggests that you explore the old house. The building is just north from the Distillery, and Njal gives you the key that you need there.

Don't forget to search the Distillery for loot. There are many bags of gold, and a chest in the northeast area holds a veritable king's ransom.

EXPLORE THE RUINS

REQUIREMENTS:	Find the old distiller's notes
OPTIONAL GOALS:	None
ENEMIES PRESENT:	Warriors and Grunts

Walk north from the Distillery and climb the hill that overlooks the surrounding countryside. There are a few warriors and a grunt at the top of the building, but that is only the beginning. A hole leads down into the house's cellar. Use the Cellar Key you were given to unlock the door. Kill the two grunts on the other side and climb to the very bottom of the house. There are two bags of gold there, along with a chest containing the Secret Recipe for flame pots!

Return to the upper part of the cellar and use the cargo net on the building's wall to get back up. Return to Njal and give him the recipe. He promises to start sending flame pots to Bodovar, at the Galcliff general store, as soon as he can. You also receive three free samples.

MEET THE MERCENARIES

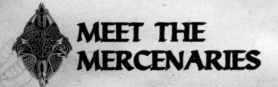

REQUIREMENTS:	Talk to the mercenaries and try to win their support
OPTIONAL GOALS:	Get some Galcliff Mead
ENEMIES PRESENT:	None

Mercenaries certainly aren't the nicest people, but their loyalty can be purchased, and the Vikings need all the help they can get. A cave of mercenaries is rumored to exist on the region's southern end. Walk out there and enjoy the view of the ocean. There is a free keg of Galcliff Mead along the way, which rewards you for taking the time to investigate this place.

Mercenary Leader Mani wants you to take out a major Legion patrol and steal all of their loot. That works for your purposes as well, but you must fulfill some conditions ahead of time. The Distillery is already under your control, so that issue is resolved. But a Watchtower along the road must fall before the ambush is launched. Look on your map to see where the Watchtower is located, and head up there next.

ALL ALONG THE WATCHTOWER

REQUIREMENTS:	Kill all of the tower's Archers and defeat their leader
OPTIONAL GOALS:	Throw as many people as possible out of windows, and get a new Leystone
ENEMIES PRESENT:	Grunts, Archers, a Berserker, and a Shaman

Leave the Mercenary Cave and move around to its northern side. There is a Leystone there, marked as Map Point 7. It's a very nice Leystone to have, because it's close to a heavily contested area that might take a few tries to defeat.

The Watchtower is at the top of the southern cliff. The road leads you directly past it, and it really is impossible to miss. Archers in the building's higher levels fire down on Skarin during his approach, and a couple of grunts patrol the road. Wade through the grunts and race up to the Watchtower to escape the archers' line of sight.

Slip to the back of the building and duel a lone berserker there. He doesn't have a chance because nobody arrives to help him, so any attacks you use are successful. Even worse for the big guy, a fast mover can get around the edge of the tower and use a stealth attack to start the fight with free damage. Furthermore, you can bash the fool off the cliffs and watch him tumble onto the rocks below! Take the Tower Key from the berserker, explore the basement on the right side for a modest amount of loot, and then return to the front of the building.

Use the Tower Key on the door and head inside. Two archers and two grunts protect the main floor. Hit the archers first, using fast attacks to bring them down and build your rage crystals. Then slam into the grunts with slow rage attacks. It's a quick fight, and it's fun.

Climb up two levels, using the ladders throughout the building, and knock all of the archers out of their positions. You couldn't ask for a more amusing sight! Then open the door on the tower's southern side.

Walk out and climb the net against the side of the building. It's a heady experience, looking out over the cliff from such a height, but try not to think about it too much. Step back into the tower at the top, and fight upward through the archers and grunts that try to stop you. Loot the chest on the higher level for a wonderful sum of gold, and keep climbing.

The top of the tower isn't easy to beat if you aren't quick about it. A shaman is on the left side when you reach the top. Like all shaman, totems protect this foe. Three archers are across from the shaman. The archers pepper your back if you go after the shaman first, so it's really better to take down the archers first.

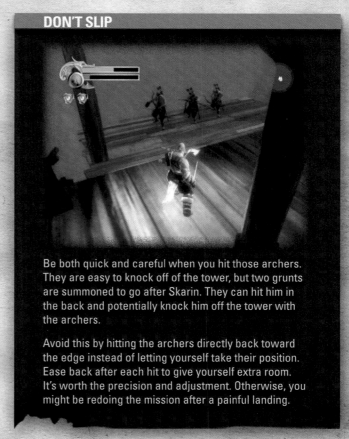

DON'T SLIP

Be both quick and careful when you hit those archers. They are easy to knock off of the tower, but two grunts are summoned to go after Skarin. They can hit him in the back and potentially knock him off the tower with the archers.

Avoid this by hitting the archers directly back toward the edge instead of letting yourself take their position. Ease back after each hit to give yourself extra room. It's worth the precision and adjustment. Otherwise, you might be redoing the mission after a painful landing.

Rip the shaman's arms off when you are done. The foul things deserve it, and the tower is clear of Legion influence when you're done.

THE AMBUSH ALONG THE SOUTHERN ROAD

REQUIREMENTS:	Slaughter all Legion forces on the bridge
OPTIONAL GOALS:	None
ENEMIES PRESENT:	Hordes of Grunts and Warriors

Your ambush is a good one. Vikings now hold the watchtower above the bridge, and the enemies will be trapped in a vice between forces on either side of the bridge itself. The Legion won't have anywhere to run and their ranks will be broken very easily.

That said, it will still be quite a fight. The Vikings are outnumbered, and heavily armored warriors support many of the enemy grunts. Buff your forces with Fire or Ice as often as possible during the encounter. Ice is even more useful here, because it helps to freeze warriors, facilitating their quick dispatch.

This ambush is otherwise a slugfest. Hang at the back if your health gets low, and use finishing moves often during army battles to keep your health and elemental energy flowing.

Return to Mercenary Leader Mani with the Battle Chest you receive. He then swears his forces to your banner!

THE CENTRAL CAVES

REQUIREMENTS:	Kill the Legion Champion in the caves and seize the area
OPTIONAL GOALS:	Find the Leystone inside the cavern
ENEMIES PRESENT:	Grunts, Warriors, and a Champion

The entrance to the Central Caves is on the complex's western side. You may already have passed it a time or two, so it shouldn't be too hard to find. Just start at Map Point 3 and walk east from there until you reach the opening.

Delayed Gratification

The Central Caves are fun to clear, and they earn you another route to the east *and* another Leystone. However, you can't fully complete the quests near the caves until the Quarry is under your control. If a bit of backtracking bothers you too much, come here later. However, coming early gets you a fair amount of money and somewhat easier transport through southern Galcliff. It's your choice.

There are many clusters of guards inside, but they aren't linked together. You can fail to ambush one, still kill them, and use stealth against future opponents. Warriors and grunts are the primary targets, usually with two to four enemies in each group.

The first major junction turns left and right. Clear the left passage first for some loot. Then search the right tunnel after you kill the lone warrior wandering there. You soon come to a stone bridge and a root-filled tunnel. A lone archer fires down at Skarin from above, but his arrows are easy to avoid.

Continue forward toward the next large chamber. Two warriors, an archer, and a few grunts are in there. Watch the patrolling warrior and wait for a good time to ambush him. The fight is much easier if you can eliminate that foe without the others intervening. Use a flame pot to soften the second warrior and his grunt buddy, and then enjoy a solid melee against the entire group.

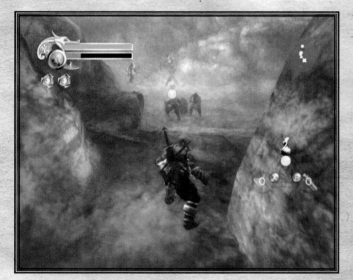

The room contains a staircase leading up and a corridor that winds off to the left. The passage takes you outside the caves, into the continent's eastern side. A small shelf follows the river back to the west.

This eventually puts you over at the Dragon Stones, and there are only three Vikings to save along the way; it's otherwise rather barren.

Skarin would be free to explore the east and have some fun, but you still have duties to address in the Central Caves.

Follow the staircase up from the large chamber once you finish exploring anything down the left side. There are a few important things above. First, a lone grunt is off working with buddies and four more patrol the corridor. Kill the first grunt and quickly move to attack the warrior and his two allies on the left. Use haste to defeat them. Then turn around to handle the returning group of grunts instead of leaving your back exposed! After the fighting, save the nearby Vikings from their enclosure.

Walk up to the Leystone in the next stretch of corridor. It's listed as Map Point 8 on the map in this walkthrough. You can return to it later if you have problems killing the champion in this cave.

The passage goes above the waterfall that you saw earlier in the cave. Carefully cross the next rock bridge, as there is very little room to maneuver. That pesky archer from before is its only guard, and he won't last beyond a single sword swipe!

Watch the brief scene as Skarin reaches the other side of the bridge. Then examine the doors on the far end. You can't open them without explosives, and you must control the Quarry to obtain said explosives. No worries, you'll have that soon enough.

Do one more thing before you leave the caves: find that champion! You're probably a little confused unless you already saw the carefully hidden route. It's all the way back in the large chamber, the one with the staircase. You might call this champion cowardly, as he let you kill all of his people while he hid up there! Can you believe that?

Look back at the entrance to the large chamber; there are small, rocky stairs and several pillars. Now examine the walls where you entered; they're covered in all sorts of vines and overgrowth. Ah, now it's becoming obvious. Don't worry if you didn't see this the first time around, as it's subtle.

Climb onto the small ledges and shuffle to the left until you reach the large rock shelves. Get Skarin up onto those, and wander around until he sees the throne room for the champion. Close in with this enemy immediately. You don't want to find him with your back toward the lethal drop!

As long as you avoid that problem, this fight is similar to those against other champions. He's big and he's tough, but you can defeat him. Take his Insignia and loot the chest at the back of the room for 600 gold pieces! Use the Cave Leystone to jump back to the west and do some shopping. Also take a moment to show the Insignia to the warriors at the Cave Camp—you know they'll be impressed.

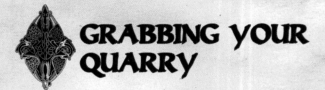

GRABBING YOUR QUARRY

REQUIREMENTS:	Free the Quarry works and take control of the area
OPTIONAL GOALS:	Get rich off the treasure that abounds in the Quarry
ENEMIES PRESENT:	Grunts, Archers, and a few Warriors

Come in from the west via the southern road. The Quarry defenders aren't fully geared to protect from that approach, so it's much easier to inflict some damage before you are seen. Kill the grunts on the road and stay behind cover as you move toward the Quarry buildings.

Optionally, you can search the area south of the road before you reach the Quarry. Three Vikings are tied to a pole there, and you can steal a moderate amount of gold from an urn and some bags in the area.

Climb the ladder at the back of the first major structure. You can assassinate two archers above, and that means fewer arrows to harass you during the main fight. Cross the wooden bridge over to the cliffs and eliminate another archer there.

Some of the grunts should soon see you. Lure them over to the side of the Quarry and kill them in pockets. A warrior should approach as well, usually with the second group that sees Skarin. Taking the Quarry in stages like this keeps you from getting overwhelmed, and the difficulty is much lower.

Next, clear the archers and grunts in the southern part of the Quarry. The archer up on the walkway is particularly nasty, as he has a great position to shoot at anyone who tries to free the Vikings from their prison. You can jump onto the boxes to the left of the archer, but he gets a chance to shoot and knock you off during the short climb. Instead, either hurl an axe at the fiend or use the small ramp on the archer's right side to get around and behind him.

With that troublesome archer gone, hurry to the Vikings' enclosure and break it open to free your allies. They clean up the rest of the fight, and you should have plenty of elemental energy with which to buff them. It's a nifty conclusion to an extremely enjoyable quest.

Scour the region for treasure. A treasure chest that you can't afford to miss is in the south. Then talk to Quarry Master Olen, as he stands very close to the chest. He will get you the explosives that you need, but first you must deal with the Eastern Cave. Olen gives you the information about how to enter the cave—there is a champion with a key.

THE EASTERN CAVE

REQUIREMENTS:	Kill a Champion, take his key, and free the Vikings inside the cave
OPTIONAL GOALS:	Get the Holdenfort Leystone before you attempt the attack, collect a treasure chest
ENEMIES PRESENT:	Grunts, Archers, a Warrior, and a Champion

This quest's primary goal is the cave at Map Point 9, but you might want to walk north and get the Leystone at Map Point 10 before you advance. It's useful to have a Leystone all the way on this side of Galcliff, and it takes only a minute to get up to the stones.

Look for a small pass between the cliffs. The Eastern Cave is located there, and the champion near the gate is the one Olen told you about. Killing him gets you the key, and there is plenty of time to rest and get your wind back before you head inside. Remember your dodging techniques, and hit the solitary champion with everything you have—he won't last.

Open the gates to the cave. Use the small wooden catwalks to get around the locked double doors across from the entrance. Three archers are in the secondary chamber, watching over the captives. A few grunts and a warrior are also below, where the prisoners are located. It's not a bad setup. Skarin has the element of surprise. Hit the archers with throwing axes to negate their utility, and climb down to engage the rest of the foes.

Break out the Vikings when the fight is over. Climb up the far ledges to open the big doors for your buddies. They march south to the Quarry, and you can leave whenever you like. However, you might want to stay and search the lower part of the first room. It looks empty, but there is a hidden chest down there—money, money!

Watch the area south of the road as you walk back to the Quarry. Three restrained Vikings are near a small cabin. Save those guys to bolster your army, and search around the cabin for even more money. You're amassing a decent stockpile again. That is certainly important, because you'll soon have access to northern Galcliff. There are more special moves to learn, and you're probably itching to see what they're like!

REACHING THE PLATEAU

REQUIREMENTS:	Save another group of Vikings, eliminate the Legion camp, and find a piece of the Dragon Gem
OPTIONAL GOALS:	None
ENEMIES PRESENT:	Grunts, Archers, and two Warriors

Get the explosives from Olen and use the nearest Leystone to return to the Central Caves. Follow the upper bridge and set the explosives in front of the locked gate at the top of the caves.

There isn't much to the Plateau Camp. A handful of grunts relax up there, but they have an archer and two warriors with them. It's hard to get any good ambush work against this team, as they are fairly close together. As soon as you start your attack, the warriors come out and play.

Hit the camp's right side first. Many of the softer targets are there, so you can eliminate more enemies with fast attacks and inexpensive rage attacks. As usual, finish the warriors last.

Break open the Vikings' cage and loot the nearby chest to complete your tasks in the area. Half of the Mugin Dragon Gem is inside the chest. The other half is presumably in the northern half of Galcliff, and there is plenty of time to find it.

YOUR FIRST LOOK AT HOLDENFORT

REQUIREMENTS:	Infiltrate the city and destroy its Barracks
OPTIONAL GOALS:	Collect Skulls and get rich
ENEMIES PRESENT:	Too many to fight

Slip over the walls on Holdenfort's western side. Skarin can climb or leap over a small gap there. You can then stealthily look over the place before the siege. Note that you can also enter via a breach in the wall along the southeastern side.

From the western entrance, use axes or the best stealth you can muster to kill the first few grunts. Take the Red Skull that you find near the fence. Walk east from there, staying among the crates and buildings to avoid being seen. Ambush and destroy the two isolated grunts along the way. Then kill an archer and a horn blower. This really limits the trouble you can get into in southern Holdenfort.

There's quite a bit of money down in the lower dock area to the east. Use the ramp in southern Holdenfort's center to get down to the docks. Ambush the warrior and grunt that patrol there. Use shoulder barges to quickly toss the warrior into the water. It's a mean way to kill such a heavily armored foe, but it sure works! Repeat this for the second warrior that comes forward soon after.

Loot the docks if you like, but don't use the ladder that leads from the northern dock section back to the main road through town. It lets you hit the warriors and their champion from the flank. That sounds like a good idea and, indeed, you can knock targets off the upper ledge, killing them quickly—*but it's very tough.* You don't have much room to maneuver, and the champion hits you almost as quickly as some of his warriors. The archers join in as well, further complicating things.

Though you can take the main bridge across, fighting two champions and a slew of their people, there are better ways to reach the far side of Holdenfort. Go to the underside of the bridge, still on the city's dock level. Hop onto the bridge's wooden framework and shuffle to the northern side without fighting a single enemy!

Climb up the dock stairs and stick to the quiet areas, away from the western road. Go far to the north and look for the almost unguarded stone steps. Climb those most of the way up, but jump down onto the grassy ramp on your left.

Jump from the ramp onto the lower, grassy ledges to your left. Use those to get closer to the western bridge. Once you get close to the bridge, you realize that you can cross the gap by leaping from support to support. This requires careful jumps, climbing, and shuffling from side to side. It's not a quick process, but it's so much easier than defeating the limitless troops that guard the direct path. The only new type of maneuver is to jump from a ledge, press away from the ledge using your movement controller, and leap across a gap while hanging. It's a neat trick!

The Barracks itself is at Map Point 11, on the bridge's southern side. Hug the walls to avoid notice, and climb onto the upper part of the building when you finally reach it. Drop the bomb by the open hatch into the structure, and get away from the place before it blows.

Now you're ready for the main assault!

CLEAN UP THE REST OF THE TRASH

Battle of the Right

Size of Battle:	Epic
Number of Stages:	Six
Enemies Involved:	Grunts, Archers, Warriors,
	a few Berserkers, two
	Champions, and several
	Shamans
Can You Use Dragons:	Yes

Stage One

The first stage of the battle for Holdenfort involves two shamans in the field and a team of enemy archers. There's always more than one way to complete these massive encounters, but one of the easier methods is to flank right and roll up the enemy line.

Do this by moving around the field's eastern side. Your troops don't come along, but there's a back way up to the eastern shaman that can't be ignored. Hop onto the rock ledges behind the eastern hills and climb the vines to reach the top. This puts Skarin behind the shaman without anything else in his way. Slaughter the shaman quickly and clean up the minimal defenders that rally to save their leader.

Immediately use the Dragon Rune you gain to plaster the archers in the west with dragon fire. This saves your forces from enduring considerable damage. There are archers in the east as well, but your troops are now arriving to fight them. Join your soldiers and buff them. Use finishing moves to build up more energy and spare health as you kill off the archers.

Come down when the hill is clear, and go after the central shaman. He isn't well defended because you've completely outflanked the enemy forces. Destroy the abomination!

An even faster and more aggressive method, if you're good at killing with elemental buffs, is to hit the first champion using the usual ice attacks. Destroy the eastern shaman with the champion's Dragon Runes. Rush the second shaman immediately afterward and ignore the western archers entirely. If you do this properly, you can end the entire stage in just over one minute, but it sure takes precision!

Stage Two

The next stage of battle focuses on the town's primary assault. Use the Dragon Rune from the second shaman to hit the main gate. This opens the way for many Vikings to engage Hel's people inside the city. It also prevents you from having to slug through *many* warriors. It's a steal for only a single Dragon Rune!

Move with your troops to hit the eastern force in the back. Then descend on the champion in the docks. This gets you another Rune. Use it on the next archer force as the Vikings move deeper into Holdenfort.

Take the fight to the next two shamans. One is down in the dock area. Fight that shaman first, as it's the closer target. Then climb the ladder from the docks up to the western tier. This gets Skarin very close to his victim without having to rush through as much of the battlefield.

Stage Three

Now you get to duel a champion on the eastern bridge. It's a fun fight, and the champion takes a few more hits than usual. He has custom armor and looks every bit the leader of Holdenfort's garrisoned troops. Thus, it'll be even more demoralizing when the archers across the bridge see you rip open his head with your blade.

It's a standard pattern for champion fighting. Perform two fast attacks, dodge back, and wait for the champion to commit to a failed swing. Then use Fafnir's Might to stun the champion, land two more hits, and dodge again. Repeat this until the poor fiend is close to death, and then close for the kill!

Stage Four

Use the Dragon Runes you accumulate to immediately kill the archers and the shaman in the far north. Then only one shaman remains, and he is on the eastern side.

Follow the press of bodies toward the northern docks. Don't try to get ahead of everyone. There are still so many enemy grunts and warriors that you'd almost certainly get killed if you went too far ahead of your forces right now.

Wait until they get all the way down to the docks. Then lead the charge against the shaman, keeping roughly apace with your troops.

Stage Five

You must dispatch two more shamans in this wave, and you don't have the Dragon Runes to take care of them quickly. That's fine. You can slice through the first shaman and use your dragon to bring down the next one. It works out perfectly that way.

Follow your troops up the large hill on the town's north side. You run into a large wall of warriors, followed by two ranks of archers and a few berserkers. Let the battle consolidate around the warriors. Hang back, doing some light fighting until there is a breach. Jump through the opening and cut through the two sets of archers.

Play a running game to avoid the berserkers. Knock the first one out of your way with a combo-ender, and hack through the shaman's totems with double fast attacks for each. Be sure to string the attacks together so that Skarin leaps from totem to totem without delay. Kill the shaman and summon the dragon to defeat its western counterpart.

Stage Six

All of the leaders within the enemy ranks have fallen. They lost their leader at the bridge, and now the last of their shamans is down. Yet there are still more than a hundred troops guarding the portal in the southwest, across the higher bridge.

Lead your troops across the bridge and let them engage the bulk of the grunts that attack. Slip into the yard where you destroyed the barracks building, and go around the inside wall's perimeter. Jump over the yellow banner against the northern side, and look where you land. It's behind the enemy grunts! Well, behind most of them anyway.

Hit the cluster of grunts in the back to make more room for your Viking allies. Then rush up the hill together. The portal is very close, and you need only a few free seconds to tap the interaction button and summon your shaman there. She needs protection while she seals off the town from Hel's powers, but that is the final stage in your conquest. Use slow rage attacks to kill off any grunts that approach, and soon Holdenfort is once again free.

A FREE CITY ONCE MORE

REQUIREMENTS:	Talk to Innkeeper Holmstein and Chieftain Honor
OPTIONAL GOALS:	Explore the town
ENEMIES PRESENT:	Only deceased ones

The Chieftain is in the northwestern part of town. He talks about all the nearby areas that need Skarin's attention. He also suggests that you speak with Shaman Asta before you head off on your own. Shaman Asta stands at the immense northern doors. She opens them once you talk to her, and she explains that a powerful clan of Vikings is in the deeper mountains. She wants you to earn their trust and loyalty.

Climb down to the city's lower tier. Look for the treasure chest that's close to the stairs. It's just a bit to the left when you come down. The new general store is across the street from that chest. You can purchase a new Health Rune there, further improving Skarin's survivability.

Holmstein is farther south, across the lower bridge. Talk to him and agree to help with his mead hall. Hand him the keg of Galcliff Mead that you found along the southern shoreline, and he rewards you well. Return later when you discover more Mead in the north. The blacksmith is across from the mead hall. You don't have any new runes to purchase there, but it's fine to pick up anything that you missed earlier and would like to buy now.

Walk all over town and loot everything you find. The Galcliff Arena is not too far away, and you need a lots of money to get everything from the ghost trainers there.

ATTACK THE BRIDGE CAMP

REQUIREMENTS:	Free the enslaved Vikings
OPTIONAL GOALS:	Get a more accessible Leystone along the way
ENEMIES PRESENT:	Grunts, Archers, and Warriors

Use the western gate to leave Holdenfort. Hit the ambushers along the upper cliffs with throwing axes, or move at high speed to avoid them. It doesn't take long to reach the Drawbridge Leystone at Map Point 12.

Fight the minimal forces near the Leystone and clear the drawbridge as well. Destroy the urn on the bridge, and use the crank next to it so that you can cross between the north and south even more conveniently.

Continue west from the drawbridge to reach the Legion's labor camp.

Don't use guile to take down this place. Rush into the middle of the enemy grunts and defy their efforts. Lay waste to the entire camp without any help, and free the Vikings when you are done. They are suitably impressed and instantly join your cause.

GET A NICE VIEW AT THE BAY RUINS

REQUIREMENTS:	Save more Vikings
OPTIONAL GOALS:	Take a look to the west and see your final goal in Galcliff
ENEMIES PRESENT:	Grunts and Warriors

Another small cluster of Legion troops is north from the Bridge Camp. They too have Vikings under their beastly guard, and you are tasked with freeing everyone. Start at the camp's southern end and use your best shield-breaking/avoiding attacks to eliminate the warriors.

Pull these enemies toward you to avoid incoming grunts. Their numbers aren't great enough to pose a major threat, even if you're casual about the assault. All the same, stay away from the Vikings' enclosure until you've defeated everything in the south. Two more warriors and a few spare grunts are near the cage, and you don't want them attacking while you still have foes nibbling on your leg.

Take the Galcliff Mead from the western side of camp and free the Vikings. Search for the modest amount of loot in the camp, and then climb up the northern cliffs.

ANOTHER WATCHTOWER? GOODIE!

REQUIREMENTS:	Seize another tactical location by killing the Archers in the northern tower
OPTIONAL GOALS:	None
ENEMIES PRESENT:	Many Archers, a few Grunts, barely any Warriors, three Assassins, a Berserker, and a Shaman

Hurry toward the tower to stay under the archers' fire. They can't hit Skarin once he reaches the tower's base, and their shots take too long to hit him at longer range. Nevertheless, their attacks look very cool against the dark and stormy sky, so glance upward just for fun if you feel lucky.

Clear the grunt and berserker from the tower's eastern side. Build up a full set of rage crystals as you do this—we'll explain why in a moment. Leap over the well on the southwestern side, and immediately use fast rage attacks to bring down the assassin that comes after you. Go directly from that fight into dealing with the berserker that charges. If you have a spare moment, kill the lone archer that supports these cretins, but this can wait if you position the berserker between you and the archer.

Leap into the basement after you recover your health and take a moment to clear your head. A grunt and a warrior jump out of the shadows to kill Skarin as soon as he walks through the door. Counter their ambush by killing the grunt immediately. Then bash the warrior against the wall and pound him with fast attacks until he's just a memory.

Take down two more grunts on your way up, and loot a treasure chest on the second floor. The third floor is another scene of complete anarchy and fun. There are many archers by the windows—they're begging you to throw them to their deaths. As always, shoulder barges are fast and perfectly suited to this task.

Climb to the fourth floor. Knock the two warriors up there over your shoulder. Do this by sidestepping as soon as you reach the top. Flank the warriors and check them over the edge to dispense with them immediately.

The next floor is a tough one. An assassin and a grunt come after you initially. Don't worry about the grunt; use fast rage attacks as soon as you can to defeat the bloody assassin. Afterward, build up rage against the grunt and prepare for more action.

CAUGHT FLAT-FOOTED

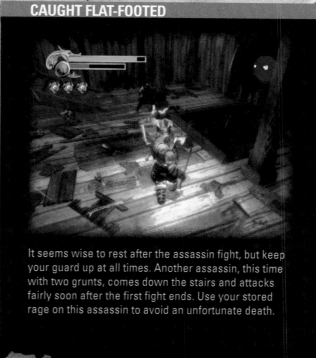

It seems wise to rest after the assassin fight, but keep your guard up at all times. Another assassin, this time with two grunts, comes down the stairs and attacks fairly soon after the first fight ends. Use your stored rage on this assassin to avoid an unfortunate death.

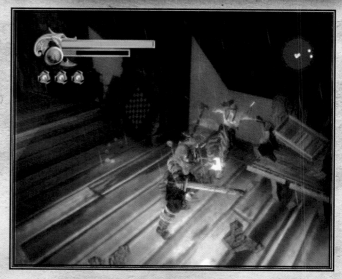

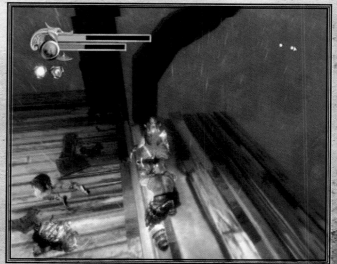

Climb some more, until you reach the very top of the tower. Four archers are on the right and a shaman is on the left. Shoulder barge all four of the archers off of their ledge as soon as you can. Then turn to counter the approaching grunts. Kill both of them and rush over to savage the shaman. It's a carefully timed fight, but sheer aggression wins out. The longer you delay, the greater the chance that something goes wrong.

Climb back down the ladders and use axes or a flame pot to kill the warriors that you avoided earlier. They can't climb up to fight, so it's a rather sad moment for them.

CLIMBING UP TO THE ARENA

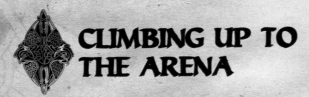

REQUIREMENTS: Liberate the Arena Camp and visit the Battle Arena
OPTIONAL GOALS: Save extra Vikings
ENEMIES PRESENT: Grunts and Archers

Look south from the Watchtower and try to spot a line of torches. These highlight a small path that heads up into the cliffs. There is another camp of Vikings to liberate up there, and you can also reach the Battle Arena to learn more moves! Take this path to the top and use axes to knock off any archers that try to thwart you.

Kill the small group of enemies at the very top and break open the cage that imprisons your allies. It's a very easy fight.

The Battle Arena is on the western side of the upper mountains. Small groups of grunts and other soft targets are here and there, but nothing appears in large enough groups to put Skarin in real danger. Look on the cliffs' southwestern edge near the Arena; a trio of Vikings is tied up there. Save them while you're in the area.

Of the new moves that are available, Hel's Fury and Valkyrie Stampede offer the most novel maneuvers. Hel's Fury gives you a *much* stronger jumping attack, and Valkyrie Stampede is unique. It's the only dodge/counterattack move in the entire game, so it's a "must buy" item as soon as you can afford it.

BEACH FRONT PROPERTY

REQUIREMENTS: Bolster your army
OPTIONAL GOALS: Get some more Galcliff Mead
ENEMIES PRESENT: Grunts and Warriors

Creep down the large hill that slopes toward the beach at Map Point 15; it's east from the Northern Watchtower. There aren't many guards down at the cliff's base, and you can free another clan of Vikings without much effort. Sneak behind the tents and ambush the patrolling troops, and then open the Vikings' cage to start the real fighting.

You might be seen before you complete this task. That won't make too much of a difference, as only two warriors and few grunts have the time to respond. The main reason to do this with stealth is to let the Viking prisoners have some fun.

Comb the beach down by the water. A keg of Galcliff Mead is there, and you find more gold as well. Look at Map Point 16 to find a beached vessel with a moderate amount of gold. You can't save most of the ship's crew, but three Vikings have survived. Cut them free once you slay the enemy berserker and his lighter troops. Another keg of Galcliff Mead is there as well!

INCOMING VIKING AT THE LUMBER MILL

REQUIREMENTS:	Capture the Lumber Mill
OPTIONAL GOALS:	Get the Lumber Mill Leystone ahead of time
ENEMIES PRESENT:	Grunts, Warriors, and a Champion

Look on your map to see where the Lumber Mill is located. It's a large area in the northeastern part of Galcliff. A Leystone is farther down the eastern coast, and it might be worth a visit there ahead of time if you'd like a safety net before you start this major assault.

All of the siege weapons in Galcliff are made at the Lumber Mill. Taking it prevents Hel from using these weapons against you. It also makes the next siege feasible when you're ready to lead the Vikings west.

There's a major entrance along the Mill's southern side, but it's well guarded and encourages Skarin to get into trouble. It's easier to come in by hopping up the western cliffs. There are only a few grunts and archers at first, and the resistance doesn't come all at once.

Stay away from the center of the Lumber Mill when you reach the top. Large enemy groups loiter here and there. You can usually see them well in advance, and there is bigger game to hunt first. Stay near the western side and follow the switchback up to the area's higher tier.

Assassinate the lone grunt on the upper hill, and wait for the champion along the road to see you. He advances for the kill, but the fight won't end as he expects. Cut him to pieces and steal the Crane Key from him.

Walk back to the western side of the hill and look over the Lumber Mill. You can easily spot the crane, and it isn't very far away! Descend the hill and avoid the large enemy group by slipping behind the building south of their position. Creep to the back of the crane and use the Crane Key to drop the Viking prisoners onto their very captors. It frees your friends and kills a number of the Legion targets.

Loot and Danger

A chest is in the Lumber Mill's northern end, behind a rundown shack. Be sure not to miss it!

Also, be careful when you collect the area's other gold bags. One of them is very close to the northeastern cliff edge. Don't leap over the fence there. A short drop and an unforgiving sea are on the other side!

Clear away the few remaining defenders, and then talk to Saw Master Bori. He waits in the champion's patrol area. He advises you that the Mill's Grinding Stones are temporarily lost. The Legion walked off with them recently, and he suspects that they are down on the beach.

You've already seen North Beach Camp, so hurry back there to get the Stones. Search the area fully, taking any of the gold that you missed earlier. The Grinding Stones are inside the camp itself, so they aren't hard to acquire. Bring the Stones back to Bori.

THIS ONE TIME AT FARM CAMP...

REQUIREMENTS:	Free Vikings
OPTIONAL GOALS:	None
ENEMIES PRESENT:	Primarily grunts and warriors

The Farm Camp is a straightforward assault. Kill the only archer in the north as you enter the area. Then directly attack the grunts and warriors. Freya interrupts to tell you that you must liberate a place of healing nearby. Otherwise, this camp is very similar to a few other targets you've hit in the north.

Release the loyal Vikings after the fighting ends. They don't have any requests to make. All of them are ready to take the fight west, as soon as your horn sounds the call to war.

WHERE IS THE VINEYARD?

REQUIREMENTS:	Capture the Vineyard
OPTIONAL GOALS:	Bring healing potions and a meal, collect a boatload of money as your reward
ENEMIES PRESENT:	Archers, Warriors, Grunts, and several Berserkers

The Vineyard is in the east, off the main road that leaves Holdenfort. However, you can't get up and into the Vineyard this way. The Legion defenders have sealed a large, wooden gate.

Walk to the east, along the hillside next to the gate. Look for a tiny path that curves up and into the hills that overlook the Vineyard. Kill a few archers on the way up, and use shoulder barges to kill the warrior, horn blower, and berserker on top of the hill.

Now that these assisting troops are cleared away, go all the way around the Vineyard and travel to the north. There is a river that flows down toward the ocean; jump up the rocks along the riverside. This takes you to the hilly area near the Vineyard.

HEIGHTS AREN'T YOUR FRIEND

Don't try leaping into the Vineyard. Even with all of the Health Runes and a good Meal, it spells your demise!

The fighting in the Vineyard gets intense if you aren't careful. Many grunts wait in reserve, and at least a couple of warriors and berserkers notice your ingress. Hit-and-run methods are very successful compared to direct action. Be ready to leave and hide in the area west of the Vineyard. You can heal there without getting much attention from the defenders above.

Fight those enemies without moving far into the farm. Build up rage crystals by slamming the berserkers with fast combos, and unleash slow rage attacks on the warriors. Normally it would make sense to fight one enemy specifically, going for the kill. But that would be a mistake here! Try to keep the enemies off of Skarin's flanks. Hit a berserker with Freya's Chariot, then nail a warrior with Fafnir's Might—good stuff!

Afterward, creep around the buildings and look for the evil horn blower near midtown. Kill him first, or his horn can bring grunts from all over the Vineyard.

As long as you succeed in downing the horn blower, everything else is easy. Just clear the path to the Viking enclosure, by the center of the area. Free the Vikings and lead them to a decisive victory. Collect all the loot and talk to Farmer Blyn. He adds some goodies to the Holdenfort store and asks you to take a letter to Archer Master Vidar.

Talk to Vidar, who stands in the western part of Holdenfort. Afterward, let Blyn know that help is on the way and will be there to defend the Vineyard. Look northwest of Blyn for a full chest of loot— you've earned it.

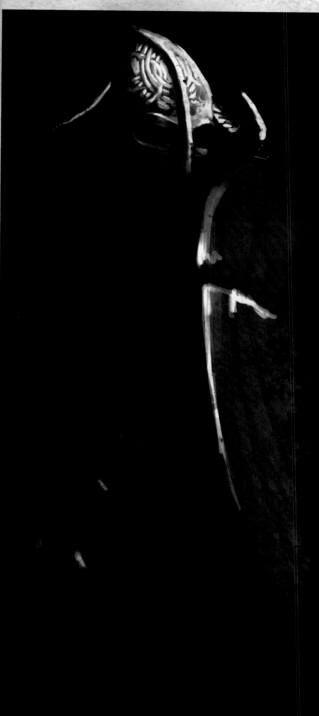

FINDING THE GUERILLA CAMP AND STEALING THE DRAGON GEM

REQUIREMENTS:	Meet the Viking clan within the Longboat Graveyard
OPTIONAL GOALS:	Pick up cash along the way
ENEMIES PRESENT:	Grunts, Warriors, and Berserkers

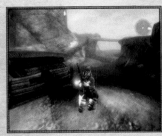

Purchase any treats from Holdenfort and drop off your kegs of Galcliff Mead to the brewmaster. He rewards Skarin quite well, giving you even more gold to work with if you still need any Health Runes or supplies.

Proceed through the large doors at Holdenfort's northern end and seek the Viking clan that Shaman Asta mentioned. They are hidden inside the Longboat Graveyard, a place with strange turns and obscured passages. Look for the urn in the first cave you reach and then climb up the western hills.

The actual Longboat Graveyard is foggy and grim looking. It's hard to see where you're going, but the path deeper into the region is to the left (west), hidden behind a set of wooden piers. Look around these piers very carefully to spot the route.

Consult your map and try to maneuver toward the southwestern part of the Graveyard. This takes you toward the path up to the Vikings' area. You're on track when you find the broken bridge. Shuffle across this span by going over the side and using the tiny ledge.

Follow the path faithfully at this point, as it stays somewhat linear for a short time. You soon reach a strange piece of ground. Something seems wrong with it, but you can't avoid stepping on the sudden grassy spot. It's a trap! But don't worry because it belongs to your potential allies. They ask Skarin to find the second half of the Dragon Gem. Doing so will prove his strength and tenacity, and they'll join his army as a result.

Climb out of the trap and walk over to the cliff's edge. The path divides, going both north and south. Turn north (to the right) and get the Leystone inside the grunt's camp. A keg of Galcliff Mead is just beside the trail where you enter the encampment.

Enter the tiny cave at the camp's eastern end. It's mostly boarded up, but you can pull a lever to activate an elevator. This takes Skarin down into the cave's lower portion. Hopefully the Mugin Gem is still there.

Explore the cave until it divides at an intersection. Follow the passage to the right, and whittle down the warriors and grunts you meet. Their numbers are small, but it's worrisome enough that they're here before you!

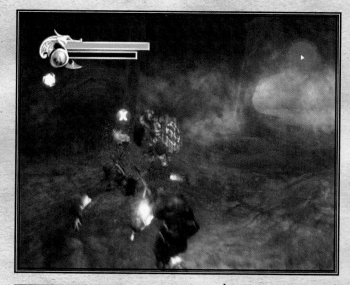

Shuffle further into the cavern and break the urn at the end of the tunnel. Turn left and look into the nearby offshoot to find a chest. This one doesn't contain treasure. Instead, it contains the Rusty Key you'll soon need—take it!

Return to the primary tunnel and follow it all the way down. Turn along the right side, going all the way back up the parallel tunnel. The Rusty Gate is at the end of the area. Open it and proceed down to the bottom of the caves. Skarin has an important encounter there. He learns that he must sneak into Caldberg.

Two berserkers and two grunts attack when the encounter ends. Dodge to gain some room at the beginning of the fight. Then focus fast attacks or Thor's Hammer on the berserkers. Kill them, waste the grunts next, and see what happens. Before long you return to the Viking's Encampment.

STROLLING INTO CALDBERG

REQUIREMENTS:	Steal the second half of the Mugin Dragon Gem
OPTIONAL GOALS:	Liberate Viking prisoners to assist in the infiltration
ENEMIES PRESENT:	Grunts, Archers, Warriors, Berserkers, Assassins, Bosses, Trained Fruitbats (Well, you get the idea.)

Take the Leystones to the area near Caldberg. Climb down the hill, south from the Caldberg bridge. Follow the sandy area across the bridge's base and ambush the warrior and his grunts down there. Alternatively, you can avoid them entirely by crossing through the bridge supports before they see you. A keg of Galcliff Mead is by the city's eastern edge, at the large watchtower's base. A single warrior guards it, and you can hit him from the back while he patrols.

Your objective is on the city's southwestern side, but don't let that guide you yet. You must first reach the top of the cliffs, and the way up is actually north, placing Skarin at exactly the *wrong* side of town, sadly. Climb the rocky switchbacks in that area, and use the cargo nets at the top to get over the walls. Only a few guards spot Skarin as he does this, and they are easily silenced.

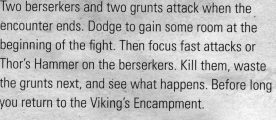

Climb a ladder on the left side of the walls. Use the bridge above to avoid a shaman and many troops in the yards below. Climb down the bridge's western steps, hopping over the last few to conceal your presence from a group of grunts with an archer. Walk a short distance south, killing a few grunts as you go; fight them on the steps to a lower part of the city.

Look for a chest of gold on the nearby rooftop. Then climb down the net on the building's western edge. Kill the grunt below, and look around the corner. Many grunts and warriors are in the next area, but there's a set of stairs on the right. Your goal is to climb them to continue infiltrating Caldberg. The easiest way to achieve this is to poke out your head, luring small clusters of troops back to your hidden cubby. Kill them there safely and repeat the process until you have a fairly clear route to reach the stairs.

If a few additional grunts spot you, don't worry about it. Keep moving, climb the stairs, and fight the grunts up there. You don't want to hang around the training yard very long! Use the tunnel north of the stairs for a quiet place. Skarin can heal there without interruption. Then, look south again and slip around the boxes that line the area. Far fewer enemies can see you this way.

Turn left against the next wall, and skirt it to reach a net that descends. More than a few enemies notice Skarin doing this nice trick. Kill most of the ones on the upper wall as you go. Then hurry down the net if you get into too much trouble. A few more warriors join at the bottom, but you'll have time to rest afterward.

It looks like you're very close to the Gem now, but appearances are deceiving. *Many* troops are stationed between this position and the Gem itself. Going directly west is tantamount to suicide. Look for the net that lets Skarin climb down onto the docks. These take him west without having to face the entire Legion!

Build up rage crystals from the lone grunts along the route. Use these to defeat an assassin on the docks' western side. Climb up the net at the docks' western end and use the boxes above for visual cover. Slip very quietly to the south and kill the last few grunts and berserkers along your way.

Look for the small western archway up top. It leads into the Gem's chamber. Rush in there and kill the distracted shaman. Then turn to fight the enemies that hurry in behind you. There aren't too many of them, and quick bursts of Thor's Hammer work quite well. Loot the chest to get the Gem Fragment and flee the city!

The way into the Crypt is east from the Holdenfort Battlefield Leystone. Climb the hills and look for a rocky bridge that leads south. This takes Skarin into the mountains, and only a few grunts and two warriors guard the way. Knock the warriors off the bridge. This gets Skarin the Key to the Crypt. Open the doors and step inside.

Follow the tunnels all the way to their conclusion, and seek a great flame there to upgrade your sword. This is the last step before you can assail Caldberg. Your army is ready. Your dragons are ready. You are ready. Return to Holdenfort to buy any items you need, turn in any final kegs of Galcliff Mead, and visit the Arena if you like. Then attack Caldberg without fear.

FINAL TASKS

REQUIREMENTS:	Summon Kelda, Talk to the Guerilla Vikings, and Have a Vision
OPTIONAL GOALS:	None
ENEMIES PRESENT:	Few

Take the Gem to the Dragon Stones and summon Kelda, a veteran she-dragon. After gaining her loyalty, use the Leystones to return to Leader Garm, of the Guerilla Vikings. He swears his blade to you! Those two tasks are quite quick, but you must fulfill a final criterion before you can begin the assault on Caldberg. Use the Leystones to return to southern Galcliff, and mark the eastern Crypt on your map. Look for Map Point 24 and start wandering down toward that region.

THE FALL OF CALDBERG

Across the Great Bridge

Stage One

The siege's initial stage takes place on the Caldberg bridge. A single giant defends the doors of Caldberg. Archers fire from either flank, and a shaman brings troops into the area to fight against your Vikings. It looks rough, but this stage is actually quite fast.

Size of Battle:	Epic
Number of Stages:	Six
Enemies Involved:	The Whole Lot of Everything
Can You Use Dragons:	Yes

Charge down the bridge with your men at the ready. Hit the initial wave of grunts and use them for elemental energy. Once you reach the giant, charge Skarin with the power of lightning, and start cutting into the huge enemy with fast attacks and slow rage attacks. Dodge when the giant raises its foot or hands, and counterattack as soon as the beast misses Skarin.

The big guy is eventually weakened enough for you to start a chain of finishing moves against it. Start the first set from the front of the beast, the second from the rear, and the third from the rear as well. None of these is timed unfairly, so it isn't too difficult to kill the giant once it's this badly wounded.

Use the Dragon Runes that fall from the giant to kill the shaman. This instantly ends the stage!

Stage Two

The doors collapse under the weight of your battering ram, and the army charges into Caldberg's eastern end. The heaviest weight of Legion troops stands right there, so it's a murderous fight. Three shamans summon their kin to war, and a mighty champion protects each one. Elemental ice is the key to winning this part of the fight safely! The champions can't survive for long against it, especially with additional Vikings hacking at them.

Kill the champion in the center first, and use his Dragon Runes on the central shaman. Kill the left flank's champion next, then the champion on the right flank. Together, their Runes can kill the shaman on the left. Skarin should be close to the shaman on the right, allowing him to defeat that foe manually.

The last shaman is on top of a wooden structure. Skarin can jump onto it and pull himself up, but enemies can knock him around during this process. Fight defensively while your Viking buddies catch up. Let them distract the enemies until you get an opening.

Climb up and knock off any berserkers that are summoned, or kill them and use finishing moves to get extra health. Use Thor's Hammer on the shaman' totems, and then slice through the boss to end the stage.

Stage Three

The siege is going well, but there are still many shamans to defeat. The next area has only two shamans. Enemy archers support the one on the left, and a champion guards the path toward the right one.

Use the champion for his Dragon Runes. Attack this boss first, and use ice to get the fastest possible kill. Burn the shaman on the right with dragonfire as soon as the champion dies. Then go after the shaman on the left. Like the last one you killed, this shaman is on top of a wooden stand. Lure his defenders away before you climb up, and stay away from the edges as you fight the shaman's berserkers.

Ignore the archers entirely. They fall back as soon as the second shaman dies, and you need every Dragon Rune you can get in this fight!

Stage Four

This is the last hurrah for Hel's troops in Caldberg. They still control about two-thirds of the city, but their numbers are beginning to dwindle. If you can pass this stage, things will dramatically improve.

Survey the battlefield and note the locations of all three archers groups. Your forces will suffer major attrition if you take too long here! Luckily, there are only two shamans, and you should have a spare Dragon Rune from the last boss you killed in stage three. Thus, you need to kill only one shaman here to get enough Dragon Runes to finish off the stage.

Go after the shaman on the right side in a direct assault. He isn't far away from Skarin's starting position. As soon as he falls, you can kill his companion from afar. Thank Odin for your dragon allies!

Stage Five

In this battle's last army phase, there are only two shamans and a single archer group on the strategic map. You must kill only one shaman and a giant to get the Runes you need to finish this.

The giant is hard to miss. He's directly in front of the enemy forces as the stage begins. Go after him with zealous fury, and rely on lightning once again to inflict extra damage. Kill the giant and use his sole Dragon Rune to torch the shaman on right (the one at the top of the stair area).

Either attack the shaman directly or go after the champion on the stairs for more Runes and the ability to end the fight with dragons. If you have substantial elemental energy, it's faster to kill the champion, but there isn't a right or wrong answer here. Use your intuition and attack the boss type that you prefer to fight!

Stage Six

Climb the steps toward the top of Caldberg. Two assassins jump Skarin on the way, but fast attacks are perfectly adequate to handle them. Build up rage crystals and elemental energy by using fast attacks and finishing moves against the assassins, and continue this trend against the archers up top.

The real fight is against Draken. He won't let you close the portal without a struggle. Give Skarin a burst of ice to start the fight, and use fast attacks and Fafnir's Might to cut Hel's great champion into quivering pieces. He can endure several times more damage than a normal champion, but his moves aren't any different than they were in Niflberg.

The only major change comes in the finishing sequence. Skarin really goes for the throat this time, and the series of moves is entirely different. The chain isn't hard to complete, but it sure is fun to watch. Galcliff is once again in Viking hands, and only the bastion of Isaholm remains in Hel's brutal grip.

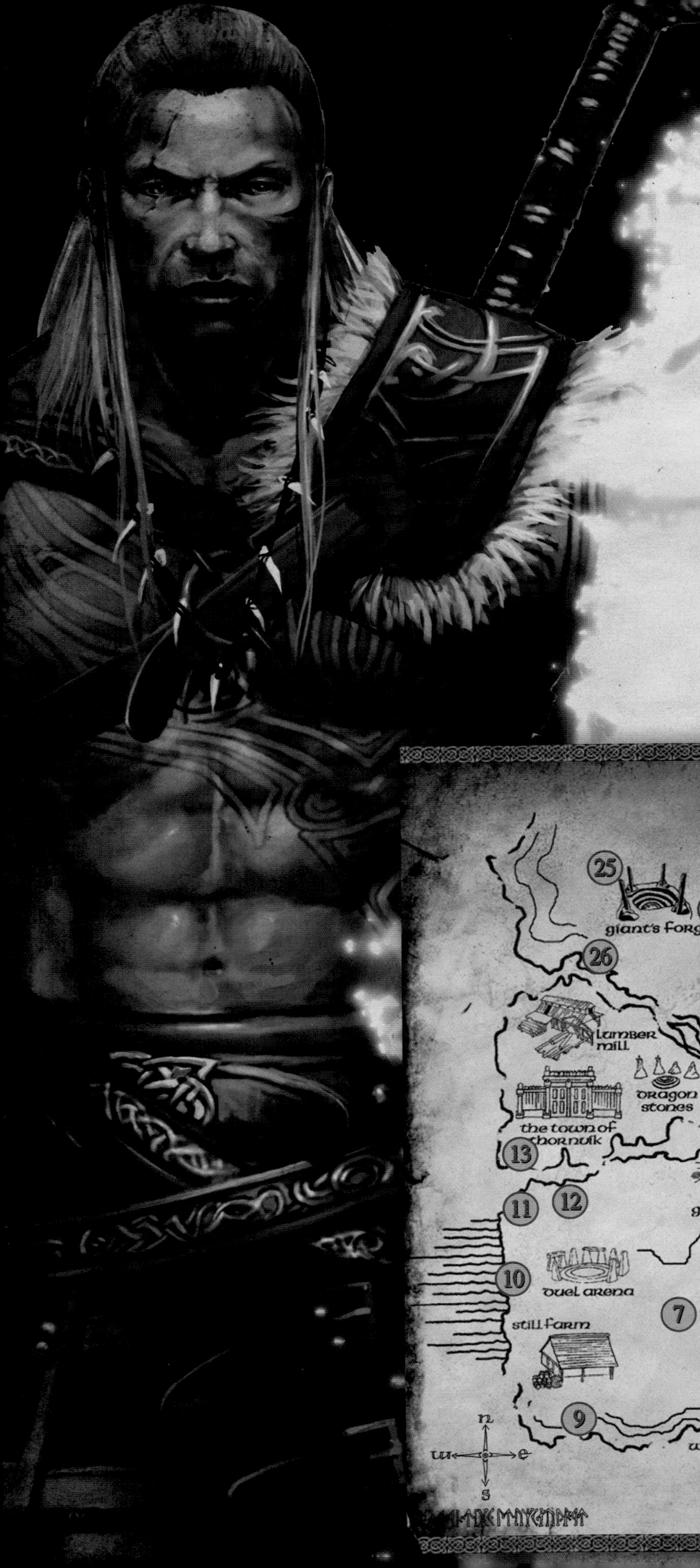

Isaholm

MAP LEGEND

1 Ingolf's Quarry
2 Farm Leystone
3 Strange Noises
4 Camp at Cold Beach
5 "Intact" Bridge
6 Viking Prisoners and Elite Patrol
7 Mountain Encampment
8 Prison Leystone
9 Distillery Leystone
10 Small Enemy Camp w/ Prisoners
11 Trio of Vikings
12 Thornvik Leystone
13 The Forest
14 Broken Bridge
15 Assassin's Cave
16 Legion Camp
17 Bridge Leystone
18 East Tower Leystone
19 Captured Vikings
20 Giant and a Keg of Isaholm Mead
21 Fenrir's Cave
22 North Camp
23 Cave w/ Mjolnir
24 Small Camp and a Leystone
25 Northwest Camp
26 Southwest Camp
27 The Traitor

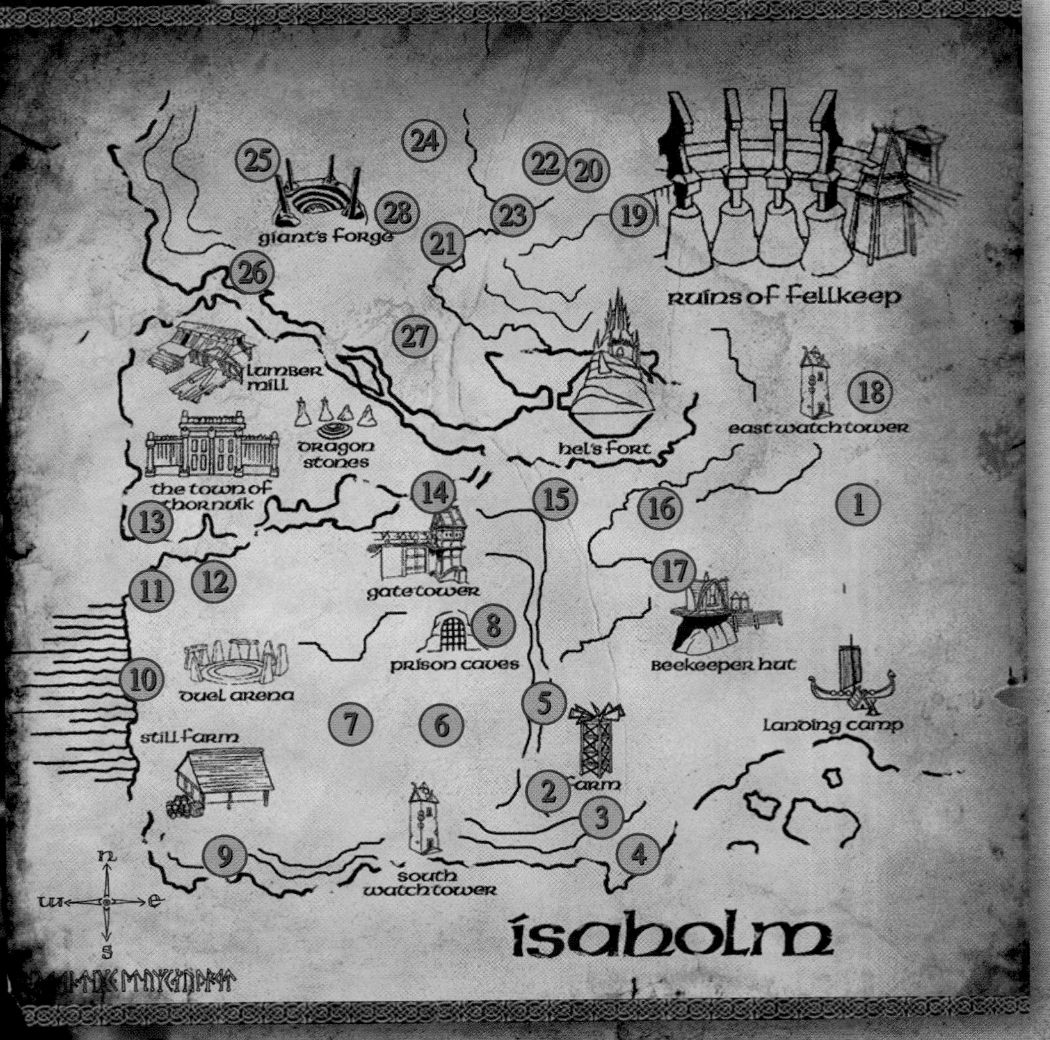

giant's forge
ruins of fellkeep
lumber mill
dragon stones
hel's fort
east watch tower
the town of thornvik
gate tower
prison caves
beekeeper hut
duel arena
landing camp
still farm
farm
south watch tower
n
w
e
s
ísaholm
1
2
3
4
5
6
7
8
9
10
11
12
13
14
15
16
17
18
19
20
21
22
23
24
25
26
27
28

THE ISAHOLM LANDING CAMP

REQUIREMENTS: Talk to Champion Osten
OPTIONAL GOALS: Shop until you drop
ENEMIES PRESENT: None

Isaholm is a harsh land. Hel's forces won't be easy to displace here, and she has concentrated some of her best leaders and monsters here. Skarin's work is certainly cut out for him.

Talk to Champion Osten, who stands at the Landing Camp's entrance. He warns you about the problems with lava floes, the presence of a nasty Watchtower, and about the loss of several important compounds.

Stop by the blacksmith to further upgrade your weapons before you leave the camp. You are now allowed to take the runes all the way up to their fourth upgrade! The general store is across from the blacksmith. There are better throwing axes there, the usual run of important map supplies, and so forth.

When you're ready to hit the road, head north and put on your game face. There is slaughter to reap!

INGOLF'S QUARRY

REQUIREMENTS: Free the Vikings and procure explosives
OPTIONAL GOALS: Try out your new elemental runes
ENEMIES PRESENT: Grunts, Archers, Berserkers, and a Champion

The Quarry is north of the Landing Camp, and it's in a geographically useful area. Nobody can reach the heart of the Quarry without making a very clear advance. Berserkers and grunts guard it. Sneak up on the initial grunts for safe kills. Then use aggressive fighting to hit the berserker and his grunts as hard as you can. Work them over to the edge and knock them off, or use low-level rage attacks to thin the herd. Both methods work well.

A single grunt walks a very long patrol out to the bridge. He joins in the fun if you take too long, but this is unlikely. You can wait for him if another ambush excites you, though advancing is probably fine as soon as your health returns.

Follow the bridge to the small chasm's far side. Make a stealthy strike on a distracted grunt by the corner. Then sneak down into the main Quarry area. Ambush a patrolling creep down there, and hit the nearby archer too.

Three grunts and an archer will likely see your attacks, but that's a very fast fight. Show off your best moves and rest for a moment afterward. The Quarry is large, and all paths forward are somewhat dangerous now. There are a few small bridges across the Quarry's lower tier. Berserkers and grunts are happy to attack you along the way, and there are occasional archers as well. Use block-checking to throw berserkers off the higher areas; it's much faster than slicing through them.

You can use the elemental energy you accrue to charge your weapons with ice to freeze the champion during your attack. This makes the fight a lot easier. Fully upgraded ice makes a huge difference. If you've upgraded a different element, try it and see what it does to even these powerful bosses.

Loot the chest in the corner and return to the Quarry's center. A locked gate prevents rescuers from casually saving the Vikings there, but you have the Key that unlocks it. Look inside, save your allies, and clean up the remainder of Hel's troops. Talk to Quarry Guard Ifor afterward. He asks for some of Im the Beekeeper's honey.

Cross the second bridge to the east to reach the Quarry's boss. Another packet of troops guards the approach, but you can easily toss them into the river below. Let Skarin heal to full health, and then approach the champion!

Alternatively, you can avoid this path by climbing down the ramp on the Quarry's west side. There are only a few archers over there. Walk across the shallow water accumulated at the bottom of the pit and get onto the docks. Climb up a series of nets the reach the top, and you reach the champion with barely any fighting at all!

This boss absorbs more punishment than the champions you're accustomed to, so don't assume much about the pacing of the fight. Use the same dodge and counterattack tricks that worked in Niflberg and Galcliff, and keep at it.

Ísabolm ● Kjarr's Farm

Look on your map to mark Im's location. Walk over there immediately, but watch the road closely. A small ring of stones lies along the route, by a copse of trees. Two assassins wait for Skarin by the stones. Build up rage crystals when you meet the occasional enemy on the road, and use fast rage attacks on the assassins to kill them quickly and safely.

Im is out in the middle of nowhere, and she doesn't have much honey to spare. Surprisingly, she still hands over some of what she has, asking little in return. Take this back to the Quarry to secure Ifor's support!

move to the farm's northern side. Kill the warriors and berserkers there to build up full rage crystals and more elemental energy. Use these resources to blow down the champion as quickly and safely as possible.

Free the Vikings and clear the rest of the valley. Kiarr is very happy to have his freedom back, but he can't lend you his earnest support until some problems in the south are investigated. He marks a mysterious spot on your map and promises to send more healing supplies to the general store back at the Landing Camp.

KIARR'S FARM

REQUIREMENTS:	Retake the farm in the name of free produce
OPTIONAL GOALS:	Try to clear the farm without resting!
ENEMIES PRESENT:	Warriors, Archers, Berserkers, a Shaman, and a Champion

Kiarr's Farm is marked on your main map. Travel to the west to reach it. The farm is essential for producing food and health supplies for the Vikings, and Hel won't let it go without a major fight. Heavily armed warriors and berserkers are all over the place. They patrol in clusters as you approach your goal. Either wait them out and avoid fighting, or hit these pockets and rest fully afterward to cut down on healing expenses.

Climb the hill that precedes Kiarr's Farm and move along the upper lip before you descend into the main valley. Kill the archers on the eastern side to clear your flank. Now, stop and look at what waits for you in the lower area. A shaman prays near an enclosure with Viking captives. A champion waits nearby, as do a few grunts. This isn't good!

Make a hit-and-run attack to devastate the shaman. Ignore all other foes and slam into its totems. Kill off the shaman and fully retreat from the encounter to shake the champion off your back. Rest to full health when you're safe, and then

Climb the hill to the south, near Map Point 3. Keep going higher until you find Idona and her gentleman friend. They aren't interested in being part of the war, but they give you a Brooch to take to Kiarr. Do so to calm the old man's nerves; he stops worrying about local problems and dedicates his farm to the cause!

THE CAMP AT COLD BEACH

REQUIREMENTS:	Kill all enemies at the camp
OPTIONAL GOALS:	Free three more Vikings
ENEMIES PRESENT:	Grunts, Archers, and Warriors

Skirt the southern hill's western edge. Look for Map Point 2 and touch the new Leystone. Afterward, go east and look for the camp at Map Point 3. A handful of grunts and warriors are there with very light archer support.

Ambush patrolling enemies on the road when they're exposed and out of sight. Take out a few targets this way, and then close in on the camp itself. Hit the southern side first, and attempt to free the tied-up Vikings there so they can assist in your attack!

Crossing the River

There aren't many safe ways across the western river. The current is too strong for even Skarin to ford, and the southern bridge has been destroyed!

Look northwest of Kiarr's Farm. There is a second bridge up there. Hel's people try to destroy that one as well, but they are rushed and nervous thanks to the defeat at the farm. They botch the job, and you can cross up there with impunity.

ANOTHER TOWER TO TOPPLE

REQUIREMENTS:	Seize the Southern Watchtower
OPTIONAL GOALS:	Save Vikings along the road and avoid the patrol
ENEMIES PRESENT:	Grunts, Archers, and Warriors

Use the northern bridge to get across the river. Five light Hel troops are in the area, but they have heavy support. Cut through them and rest for a moment. Note the dangers along the road ahead. An elite patrol is close by, wandering along this region's northern stretch. Stay close to the mountains for now, and search for a trio of imprisoned Vikings close by. Wait for the elite patrol to pass before you slip south and head for the Watchtower.

Kill the warriors and grunts outside the tower first. Look on the side of the building for the basement entrance and jump down there. Rip through two more grunts and a warrior. Then start climbing toward the top. Resistance is much lighter than you've come to expect in these buildings—be thankful!

Open the chest two floors from the top to get a treat, and then finish clearing the tower. This Watchtower is easier than most. There aren't any bosses, and none of the fights has many enemies. Just avoid getting thrown out of windows!

NYDI'S DISTILLERY IS THE PLACE TO BE

REQUIREMENTS:	Free another clan of Vikings and get the old still up and running
OPTIONAL GOALS:	Get the Distillery Leystone
ENEMIES PRESENT:	Grunts, Warriors, Berserkers, and a Champion

The Distillery is on Isaholm's western side. Its defense is based on a numbers game. Hel has stationed a slew of her light troops in the area. Freya wants you to use flame pots to thin their ranks, and this is a viable option.

However, there are other ways to do the job. Approach the camp's eastern edge and draw off warriors and berserkers. You can then kill them in manageable packets. Nidhogg Strikes and Fafnir's Might still work wonders.

This early fighting takes place without drawing reinforcements. You are free to withdraw and rest afterward, then slip back in quietly. You can make it all the way to the Viking pen without being seen on your second run. Free the Vikings from their enclosure and buff them with elemental might. A champion is around the corner, in case that influences your choice of which element to use.

Many Vikings are trapped at the Distillery, so the battle turns decisively in your favor once they are free. The champion gets obliterated quickly, and the remaining enemy troops are doomed before they can do any harm. Talk to Distillery Nydi after the commotion dies down. He wants to ambush a Legion patrol and, by great Odin's beard, you will help him.

Though it's out of the way, take some take to leave the Distillery by traveling north. Jump down the gentler hill sections up there and continue northwest until you find Map Point 9. This is the Distillery Leystone, and it really comes in handy. You can pop back to town to spend some money and supply before you start the ambush!

AMBUSH POINT

REQUIREMENTS:	Destroy the Legion patrol
OPTIONAL GOALS:	Save a trio of Vikings to the south
ENEMIES PRESENT:	Grunts, Berserkers, and Warriors

The Legion grunts knew they were in trouble when they were assigned to "Ambush Point." The place gives one the sense that life is short and dangerous. Start the encounter at your leisure, but first consider buying a meal and a potion or two. Also, you can spend some time running around the region, clearing other enemies and accruing more elemental energy. It's not mandatory, but you can start the ambush with a full bar and really stick it to your enemies.

No matter what you do, the fight is frantic and brief. Both sides have high numbers, and everyone meets moments after the cut scene ends. You start at the back of the enemy force. Most Vikings are on the right side, and you get to carve your way toward them. Many targets are comparatively light, though a few berserkers are in the mix. Lightning lets your people sow a line of destruction through the Legion.

Remember to back off and find room to breathe if you take too much damage. If you're worried about getting overrun, move toward the other Vikings and use defensive moves: blocking, dodging, Thor's Hammer, and short combos.

Mastering Your Skills

You probably have a fair sum of gold again. That means it's time to see your trainers at the Arena. Mark its location on your map. Climb the path at the Distillery's northwest side. Odin's Doom upgrades your slow jump attack; Might of Valhalla is insanely good against shield users and high-health targets; and Curse of Fenrir works wonderfully against groups.

Three captured Vikings are on the western side of the same mountain. They sit on a rocky shelf, covered by a single grunt and an archer on a separate platform.

When the battle ends, search the southern lowland for Viking prisoners. Three men are tied up down there. Free them after you kill the nearby warriors and berserkers.

Walk west, through the remainder of the lowlands, and free another trio of Vikings. They're southwest of the Distillery. Liberating this part of the country doesn't mean much in the larger conflict, but it's a nice thing to do.

WANDERING INTO THORNVIK

REQUIREMENTS:	Steal the Key to the Prison Cave
OPTIONAL GOALS:	Get a feel for the city before you besiege it
ENEMIES PRESENT:	Grunts, Warriors, Archers, and Berserkers

Swing wide of the mountains and travel north, toward Thornvik. The city is under heavy enemy control, so this mission is a stealthy one. Find Map Point 11 and go there ahead of time to climb the rock shelves and rescue a few more Vikings. Then it's time for the real heroics!

Skirt Thornvik's edge and ignore the drawbridge and the main gate. There is no way to get inside that easily…not for now, at least. Instead, look for the stone platforms on the city's eastern side. These rocks have survived the lava floes that run under the city. Leap between them and claim the keg of Isaholm Mead that's abandoned there. This route lets you jump in through the back of the city.

Follow the road's contours, going south at first, then turning west into the city's center. A treasure chest is there, but toss an axe into the nearby archer to grab it without disruption.

Mixed groups of warriors and grunts are in the streets. They never attack in large numbers because the city is in such a state of ruin. Hel has destroyed Thornvik so thoroughly that her own minions can no longer defend it.

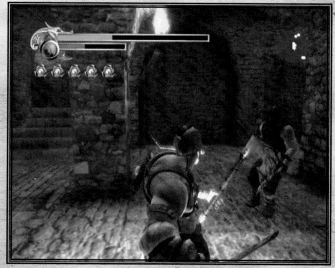

Sneak up the city's western side, and stay behind buildings there as much as possible. An open section in front of the bridge hosts more than two dozen troops. Reinforcements appear there from time to time, so you can't clear it for long.

Come around the edge of the western buildings and hurry onto the bridge. Only some of the enemies follow. You can clear them away on the other side. Knock some into the lava and use traditional attacks on the remainder. You can't trash enough enemies to get time to rest, so use a potion after this if you take too many hits.

Your objective isn't far away. You can see the large tower from a fair distance, but don't go inside until you kill or shake off any pursuers. The enemy inside is in the basement. He's a tough adversary, fighting defensively throughout the encounter. Back off and lure him into aggressive attacks. Then counter with rage attacks until he resumes defending himself.

Kill the disgusting cur and take the Prison Key from his body. Leave the city and go back to the Distillery. The Prison Camp isn't far from there.

THE MOUNTAIN ENCAMPMENT

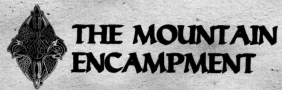

REQUIREMENTS:	Kill all targets in the area
OPTIONAL GOALS:	None
ENEMIES PRESENT:	Grunts, Archers, and Berserkers

Look north, along the hills that lead up into the mountains. A small encampment of troops is there. They don't hold anyone captive, so it's not an especially important objective, but you must reach the Prison Cave beyond, and it would be foolish to leave enemies at your back.

Climb the hills and take out the archers first. They're stationed along the ridgeline, and they're a huge problem if you leave them alone. Afterward, you must defeat berserkers and a few grunts.

Rage attacks are essential here because there are so many high-health enemies. There aren't any high places to knock enemies to their deaths, but you can toss foes off the hills to buy extra time against groups.

Kill everything you see and scour the area for stragglers. The camp is yours and you can proceed to the Prison Cave.

PRISON CAVE

REQUIREMENTS:	Save your people
OPTIONAL GOALS:	Find the Prison Leystone
ENEMIES PRESENT:	Grunts, Warriors, Assassins, Berserkers

The Prison Cave's entrance is on the other side of the hill. Go through the narrow gap beyond the Mountain Encampment, and hug the cliff to the right. This lets you sneak up on a warrior and two grunts outside the next cave. Ambush them by killing one grunt immediately and savaging the next with a rage attack. Move toward the mountain, drawing the warrior over to you. Then block check the poor guy off the cliff's edge—see you later, pal!

Rest outside the cave until you reach full health. Be mindful of a falling assassin when you look into the first cavern. The attacker might land on your head, but it can't kill you by itself. Shake off the wretch and pound him into the wall.

Stay around the corner and watch for the next enemy to turn around. It's a patrolling berserker. Use a stealth attack for a free kill, and then keep walking. The path splits, going left or straight. The left passage holds some gold, but the straight path leads you toward the prisoners.

There are many opportunities for stealth kills. Move slowly, rotate the camera around corners to watch enemies without revealing your presence, and lay waste to the grunts and warriors in your path.

The next large chamber features very solid fighting. Multiple grunts and warriors attack once they see you. Fight them out in the open and use level-two fast rage attacks (Nidhogg's Strike) to murder the warriors. Use the grunts as rage-builders, and don't advance past the large door during the action. The room's far side has a Leystone, but three berserkers stand there. Don't walk over to them until you're clear of other distractions!

Open the large prison doors after you kill the berserkers. Cross the bridge on the other side, staying behind cover to score a few stealthy kills. An urn filled with gold is on the bridge's right side, but the path you need is on the left.

Climb the ramp there and knock off the three archers above. A few warriors protect the crank that releases the prisoners. Use the strongest slow rage attacks you have to break through these enemies, and knock the survivors off their ledge. Turn the crank and set loose the last of the men in the south. It's time to lay siege!

JUSTICE FOR THORNVIK!

Lay Siege to Thornvik

Stage One

The battle for Thornvik isn't nearly as long or as grueling as the battle for Holdenfort. Hel has been caught slightly off guard, and her minions haven't fortified the city well enough to withstand a full Viking siege!

Nevertheless, she has devoted five shamans to Thornvik's defense. There are also a few giants, a champion, and plenty of lesser troops to sell their lives on this field. Bring them down.

Size of Battle:	Large
Number of Stages:	Three
Enemies Involved:	Everything!
Can You Use Dragons:	Both Dragons

Survey the initial battlefield before you commit to either flank. A shaman is on the left with a champion as its defender. This is perhaps the closest and most accessible major target.

A team of enemy archers defends their shaman on the right side. That's a very solid choice for your secondary target.

A shaman is up on the city's walls in the center. You can't reach this foe without circumnavigating the town and coming in from the back. You'll have very little support if you do this, and there are much easier ways to exterminate that sucker.

Flank left and bowl into the champion and his troops. You can try to avoid this champion and kill the shaman on the dark hills beforehand, but it's a risky gambit. Better to make a clean run. Cut through the ground troops on your way toward the champion, and use finishing moves often to build elemental energy. Buff Skarin and the troops with ice, and try to roll over the champion without a huge investment of time or health.

Climb toward the shaman when the champion falls. Avoid getting into too heavy a fight with nearby defenders; skirt around them using single fast attacks and Thor's Hammer to clear away anything that you can't avoid. Murder the shaman and use the second Dragon Rune you gain to summon the dragons against the central shaman. This removes a major thorn in your army's side.

Roll into the center, hitting the enemy forces there from the back. Build more elemental energy as you go, and use lightning to support your attack on the giant in midfield. Use fast dodging, and don't be overly ambitious. You should make good time here, and the strategy is sound. Don't let the stress of battle make you to fight too aggressively against the giant.

You have a choice when the giant falls: Blasting the eastern archers makes it easier to hit the last shaman without problems. It also spares your forces a few more casualties. However, this prevents you from going into the siege's second stage with a full set of Dragon Runes…and you need them.

So, you can take out the archers with dragonfire if you like, but the conservative player might wish to hold back the attack for now and build up even more strength by doing the work manually.

Either way, the eastern shaman is your last serious target in the first stage. It doesn't have any major defenders, and the fiend's position is fairly exposed. Go send it back to Hel!

Stage Two

The second stage takes place east of Thornvik. A major column of troops has come down from the eastern mountains and is ready to hit the Vikings from the rear. You must act quickly to prevent your forces from getting caught in a vice and slammed against the walls of the very city they intend to siege.

Use your Dragon Runes immediately. Take down at least the two archer groups on the city's walls. Also bring down the archers high to the east if you saved a third Dragon Rune.

Then it's time to blast the two giants that dominate the enemies' ground troops. Thankfully, they aren't close enough to each other to provide support, so you can pick off each giant without extra trouble. You have much more elemental energy for the first giant, but the second target is still relatively safe if you use your slow rage attacks well and keep slapping down the damage.

Use the Dragon Runes from the first giant to kill the shaman on the right; he's the more obnoxious one to go after. Hit the other shaman with the Dragon Runes from the second giant.

This stage is sudden and scary, but skilled dragon use turns it into a one-sided victory for the Vikings.

Stage Three

There isn't much left besides the rank-and-file troops inside the city itself. The dragons blast open the route for your troops to center Thornvik, but you must cleanse the portal to finish the siege. Look on your map and move toward the bridge that divides northern and southern Thornvik. The portal is directly in front of the bridge, so it's easy to find when you know where look.

Stick with your troops to avoid getting overwhelmed. As always during large fights, build up your energy as soon as you can. Summon Shaman Asta at the portal, and use ice energy to protect her from the enemy troops that spawn. It takes her a minute to completely sever the connection with Hel, so stay vigilant. Fast attacks and low-level slow rage moves do the trick just fine.

And with that final blow, Thornvik is free once more!

MEETING THE PEOPLE OF THORNVIK

REQUIREMENTS:	Talk to the Chieftain and Innkeeper Valin
OPTIONAL GOALS:	Do some extra shopping
ENEMIES PRESENT:	None

The Chieftain and Innkeeper of Thornvik are both in the city's southern section, along with the Leystone that you use as your future default. Talk to Valin and deliver subsequent kegs of Isaholm Mead to him for a princely sum of gold. The Chieftain is northwest of the inn, and he apprises you of the situation in northern Isaholm. It's not surprising to learn that the situation is bad. After all, this is the strongest bastion of Hel's power and influence in Midgard.

The Chieftain gives you Travel Papers to show to the guards at the northern gates. Take care of any shopping that you wish to do before you depart. The blacksmith is on the northern side of town, just across the bridge. The general store is also in the north, and it's fairly close to the city gates.

Show your Travel Papers to the guards in the north and set your sights on the Lumber Mill. Freya wants siege weapons, and you have every reason to please her.

TAKE THE LUMBER MILL

REQUIREMENTS:	Release the Vikings and kill all enemy troops in the area
OPTIONAL GOALS:	Get extra money from the west
ENEMIES PRESENT:	Grunts, Warriors, Berserkers, a Shaman, and a Giant

Search the area west of Thornvik before you attack the Lumber Mill. You don't find huge sums of the money out there, but a spare urn and a few gold bags can sure help you a little!

The Mill is north of town, and it's not very far at all. Expect berserkers and warriors in fair numbers, and tougher creatures are in the area as well. Stay on the compound's southern side and kill off the weaker troops. Lure as many as you can down to your position and heal after the fighting.

A shaman is on the camp's west side and a giant relaxes on the eastern side. Kill the shaman first, as it can summon reinforcements to an already tough fight. Luckily, the two are far enough apart for you to eliminate them without both harassing you simultaneously.

Take out the shaman and back off. Some extra enemies come forward to catch you, and the distance prevents you from getting overloaded. Look for the horn blower in camp. Cut him in half as soon as possible. In some ways, that guy is more dangerous than the bosses. Don't let him call for help, whether it costs you a spare axe or even a flame pot.

Kill the giant when the fight at the Mill stabilizes, and release the Vikings from their pen afterward. They can clean up the remnants of the Legion troops.

Look for Lumber Master Beck when the dust clears. He's eager to produce weapons of war to strike back at Hel, but he doesn't have the materials that his camp needs. The forest to the south has plenty of lumber, but there are still too many Legion troops down there for him to avoid. It seems that the Forest is your next target.

Look on the camp's north side for a treasure chest before you set forth. Leaving behind that much money would be such a waste. There is also an urn not far south from there—get that too.

KNOCK, KNOCK

REQUIREMENTS:	Open the doors of the Gate Tower
OPTIONAL GOALS:	None
ENEMIES PRESENT:	Grunts, Archers, Warriors

SURPRISE IN THE WOODS

REQUIREMENTS:	Clear the Forest
OPTIONAL GOALS:	Let the Horn Blower do your work
ENEMIES PRESENT:	Grunts led by a Horn Blower and a Berserker

The enemies are spread out in the southern forest, and it takes a while to round them up. You can carefully use stealth attacks to kill almost all of them. They patrol, leaving their backs exposed so often that you might even finish the quest without having to defend against a single attack.

A faster and more exciting approach is to use the Horn Blower near Map Point 13 to gather the troops for you. This makes for a tougher fight, but it's no worse than you've faced at most of Isaholm's objectives. Plus, it spares you from hunting down the rest of the foes.

The group's last enemy has the Insignia you need. If you have any trouble finding this guy, he's usually the one along the cliff's edge in the very southwest. Knock him off and wave goodbye to the poor fool. Take the Insignia back to the Lumber Mill.

Skarin can't open the gates to the east of Thornvik from the ground. They're huge, and there is obviously a mechanism somewhere else that allows people to open the path. Hel's forces suffered a major defeat at Thornvik, but they managed to close the gates in time and hold that part of the pass.

It's time to outthink them. Take a path that the enemies haven't planned for; use the Gate House's upper reaches to open the doors. Look for Map Point 14, southeast of the Dragon Stones. Small, wooden bridges once reached across the mountain gaps. Smart Legion troops have destroyed these bridges, but Skarin can still leap across carefully.

SURVEY AND SLAUGHTER BEFORE YOU JUMP

Kill the nearby warriors, archers, and grunts before you attempt any of these leaps. Getting struck or shot out of the air over a major drop is a *bad thing*.

You've done it many times before, but don't forget to knock warriors off the high cliffs if you desire quick kills without much work. Warriors defend themselves vigorously, and they just beg for this treatment.

Cross the bridge with careful jumps, using throwing axes against the archers on the far sides. Sidestep over the small planks deeper into the mountains, and before long you reach the Gate House. The crank you need is on the compound's southern side, and it's barely guarded. The siege on Thornvik cleared out most of the troops from this area. As soon as the doors open, the Viking seize the Gate House and it stays under your control.

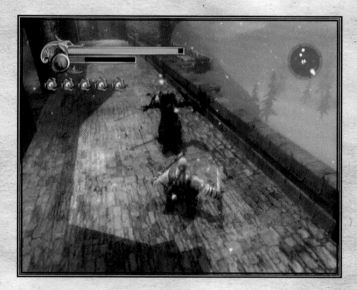

 Travel east, through the gates, and chase after the grunt that spots you on the path. He runs to his buddies at a small bridge, but the five of them together are nothing against you. If you can, take out the archers at the far side first, and don't worry about falling into the water. It's *way* too shallow to hurt. You can't toss the warrior or berserker in there either; they just get back up and return to the fight.

A small cave on the path's north side holds an urn full of gold, and you have to kill only one assassin to earn it. Loot the place if you're looking for money—it's listed as Map Point 15.

Three tied-up Vikings are also south of the small bridge. Free them when you get a moment.

TAKE OUT THE CAMP

REQUIREMENTS:	Kill all Legion troops
OPTIONAL GOALS:	Discover the southern Leystone
ENEMIES PRESENT:	Archers, Grunts, and a Berserker

The path divides into a northern route and a southern route shortly after you pass the bridge. Choose the northern stretch first and follow it down into the lowlands. There is a camp there, marked as Map Point 16. Kill the troops there, and use your axes or a fast rush up the eastern hills to kill the archers that fire at you. This clears the camp, but continue south and get the Leystone at Map Point 17.

Clear the small cave beside the Leystone of its gold and its lone berserker. For even more loot, keep following the southern path all the way around the mountains. You don't find more enemies, but a keg of Isaholm Mead is at the cliff's end!

Return all way to the divide by the small bridge. Follow the southern route this time to advance on the East Tower. The path leads to a much larger bridge. High-tier fast rage attacks work very well here because they tend to push one or two enemies off the edge without much fuss.

Cross the bridge and save the Vikings on the road's northern side. Just a few warriors and a berserker guard them. Three more Vikings are just south of the East Tower. Free them too, and then begin your attack on the Tower itself.

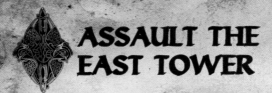

ASSAULT THE EAST TOWER

REQUIREMENTS:	Blind Hel's watchmen by freeing the Vikings and seizing the watchtower
OPTIONAL GOALS:	Search the surrounding area for additional threats
ENEMIES PRESENT:	Grunts, Archers, Warriors, and Berserkers

Look to the west of the tower for a small cave. Search that for extra money and a free kill. But it's obvious that the tower itself is the real target. Climb the hill beside the road and approach the tower. A few heavy troops stand outside, getting some weapon practice—you can kill them easily. Lure them behind the rocks if you wish to avoid archer fire.

The tower's guardians have learned from previous mistakes. They've secured the entrance down into the basement, and the front door is properly locked and reinforced from within—so much for the easy route. Look on the building's western side for a Leystone! Walk past that to discover the important location, and then retreat to the small northern hill that sits beneath the tower. Climb the hill and kill the guards by the rope bridge up top.

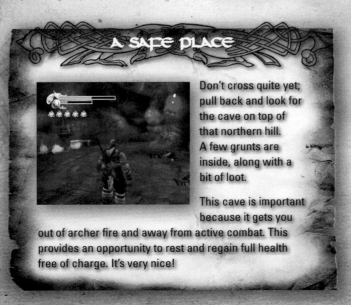

A SAFE PLACE

Don't cross quite yet; pull back and look for the cave on top of that northern hill. A few grunts are inside, along with a bit of loot.

This cave is important because it gets you out of archer fire and away from active combat. This provides an opportunity to rest and regain full health free of charge. It's very nice!

Leave the cave when you're ready. Cross the bridge and climb two levels of the tower. A berserker and a handful of archers are on that tier. There aren't many big walls there, so it's very easy to knock enemies to their deaths. Clear away these minions and search the treasure chest on this level for the East Tower Cellar Key.

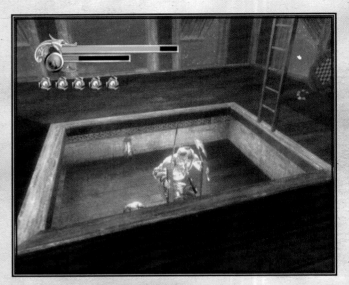

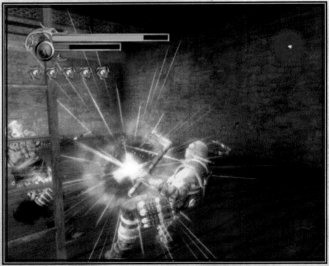

Retrace your path and climb all the way down the tower, past where you entered. There are several levels of guards, but each floor has only a few targets. If you want to save time and can spare a small amount of health, hop down instead of climbing; it's dangerous only if you are close to death.

Unlock the cellar door when you reach the bottom, and escort the Vikings inside back to the main floor. They rush out and organize their own patrols of the area. Legion troops can no longer come and go as they please.

A VISIT TO FELLKEEP

REQUIREMENTS:	Investigate Fellkeep and speak with its survivors
OPTIONAL GOALS:	Free Vikings in the wet lowlands beneath the Keep
ENEMIES PRESENT:	Grunts, Berserkers, and a Giant

Fellkeep is a massive fortress with geographic barriers that are a dream of every military leader. Impassable cliffs block entry from the north and east. A steep drop-off into wet lowlands prevents easy access from the west and south, and only a single bridge grants normal access to the Keep itself.

It sounds like a perfect place to defend, but even here Hel's troops have had considerable success. The Keep has not fallen, but its walls are damaged and the defenders are weary, hungry, and hard pressed.

Cross the bridge into the keep and search for Shaman Asta. She has a very important conversation with you. This ends with her pointing out the Shaman's Cave, down in the lowlands. Go there as soon as you've discovered the Leystone only a minute up the road from Asta's position.

Leave the Keep and slip down the eastern hills into the lowlands. Save the Vikings at Map Point 19, as they are on your way and could use the help. Continue west and watch the giant in that region. A keg of Isaholm Mead is north of the giant's position. Attack the giant, but keep an eye on your flank. Several grunts join the encounter, so break away from the giant to slam each grunt with a fast attack and Thor's Hammer. Then finish killing the giant. You can rest after it falls.

Open the locked door to the Shaman's Cave and collect the Herbs from a treasure chest. Asta marks the fire cave to the east. You can't use the upper bridge out of Fellkeep; that bridge is still out of commission.

Instead, leave Fellkeep the way you entered. Walk overland to the west and enter the next Cave at Map Point 21. The long strip of land leading to the Cave passes just north of Hel's Fortress, so you get your first really good look at the place. Shake your fist at it a few times if you like, but be on guard. Archers, grunts, and warriors are on the trail. They're modest nuisances, but you get to save three Vikings before you reach your objective.

Use a stealth attack to hit the group inside the front entrance. Knock the rest into the lava with block checks, and be done with the whole lot. Loot the side tunnels for substantial gold. Then cross the lava pit via the small ledge on the left.

Circle around the edge of the burning chamber beyond, and burn your Herbs at the bottom of the pit. Then return to Shaman Asta to learn the significance of these acts.

Talk to Shaman Asta and get permission to use the upper bridge leaving Fellkeep. You can liberate three more Viking clans out there, and you need better weapons and the final Dragon Gem.

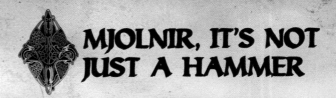

MJOLNIR, IT'S NOT JUST A HAMMER

REQUIREMENTS:	Get the final Dragon Gem
OPTIONAL GOALS:	Loot the extensive cave network for considerable wealth
ENEMIES PRESENT:	Grunts, Archers, Warriors, Berserkers, Assassins, a Shaman, and a Giant

THE NORTH CAMP

REQUIREMENTS:	Slaughter the camp's defenders
OPTIONAL GOALS:	None
ENEMIES PRESENT:	Grunts with a Horn Blower, Warriors, and Bersekers

The North Camp is located at Map Point 22. Three Vikings are kept as hostages there, and a moderate assortment of enemies defends the region. Grunts, warriors, and berserkers patrol the grounds, and one of the grunts is a horn blower. Look for him first and kill him at range to prevent the whole group from swarming.

Clear the enemies near the camp's eastern side and free the trio of Vikings. After that, it's a simple battle without major risk.

Run along the line of mountains leading west. A tiny cave hosts three Vikings to save, but that isn't your primary goal. The Cave at Map Point 23 leads into an extensive network of tunnels. Myriad forces are inside the corridors, and you must face two powerful bosses before you can loot the place. Yet, it's worth your time in every way to go there now. The final Dragon Gem is hidden deep within the Cave, and Mjolnir allows you to summon a third dragon to aid your army.

Follow the stone bridge that leads south and into the cave complex. Be alert for archers along the way. Rush them and use jumping attacks to clear these foes without breaking your momentum. Barrel into the tunnels and start clearing the top floor. Use your mini map to figure out where to go; there is treasure everywhere, and you can access areas that you haven't been by seeing where the bags of loot pop up. It's a very useful trick.

At first, there are *many* opportunities for ambush attacks. You can kill enemies facing the wrong way without a struggle. Build up a full set of rage crystals and save them for now! You don't encounter major challenges until you reach the large, open cavern at the back. You enter on the upper tier. A bridge hosts a shaman on the far side, but you can ignore him initially.

Open the chest behind the giant to take Mjolnir, the final Dragon Gem. Next time you are close to Thornvik, head out to the Dragon Stones and summon your last flying ally! Bid Bolthor to awaken. This mighty dragon is a tremendous boon when war dawns on Hel's frontier.

ISOLATING THE GIANT'S FORGE

REQUIREMENTS:	Eliminate the series of camps that support the Giant's Forge
OPTIONAL GOALS:	Find a Leystone close to the Forge
ENEMIES PRESENT:	Grunts, Warriors, Berserkers, and a Shaman

Several camps of enemies are near the Giant's Forge, in the northwestern part of Isaholm. The best way to get a clean strike on the Forge is to get the Leystone at Map Point 24 and circle the region, destroying all the camps before closing in on your primary target.

Only a few grunts and warriors are near Map Point 24. They're chumps compared to Skarin's might and fury. Toy with them for a short time and then release them back to Hel's gentle care.

The second camp is near Map Point 25, and it's a far tougher place to assault. A shaman leads the grunts and warriors there, and the shaman can call in berserkers. It's a bad situation. Don't attack the grunts or warriors first. Either swing wide of the whole camp and free the Vikings to the west, *or* hit the shaman first, killing the leader before pursuing its troops.

When you destroy the shaman's totems, be careful of the berserkers; they are the only foes worth stopping to kill. Turn, hit them once, and use Thor's Hammer as a follow-up. That should kill them every time and leave you free to demolish the totems. The shaman shouldn't survive more than two summoning sessions!

Instead, move to the side and look for a descending tunnel. Loot the chest you pass, and move toward the end of the passage. There is a second chest, but you must face an assassin's ambush before you can get to it. Be ready to face this foul enemy and wiggle away from him. Now is the time to unleash the rage crystals that you held in reserve, killing the assassin almost instantly with a level-two or level-three fast rage attack!

Open the assassin's chest to get the Key you need, and then return to the shaman. Kill this isolated boss and unlock the door behind it. Walk down to the complex's deepest level, and sneak around the stones, killing the few grunts down there. Don't approach the giant until it's the last living enemy in the room. You can retreat to heal before you fight the giant. Do so if you're low on health or if you're still shaky about destroying these massive beasts.

The last camp is at Map Point 26, in the south. You can't easily free the Vikings in that area beforehand, but the fighting is very easy. There aren't any bosses, and the grunts and warriors aren't organized. Kill their horn blower for an easier fight, but even a massive rush is survivable.

Lure the enemies over to the southern ledge, and knock them over if you have any trouble. Break open the Vikings' pen when you're done, and speak with Warrior Kuan. He tells you of foul actions that cannot go unpunished. Note the new location on your map, and immediately travel east to exact justice.

Search for a Viking among the enemy forces at Map Point 27. Berserkers and warriors are there, in addition to the traitor. Kill those targets first. They are faster to defeat and they don't fight as defensively, especially the berserkers.

Use Valkyrie Stampede to dodge and counterattack the traitor. Might of Valhalla, the level-three slow rage attack, is also very good at slamming this skilled fighter. Let him expose himself with failed attacks that you either block or dodge, and then use fast attacks to build rage.

Take the Traitor's Shield when the evil Viking dies and bring it back to Warrior Kuan. He then swears loyalty to your banner!

Go to Map Point 28 and make one more camp fall. Sneak up to the cage and kill the nearby grunts and berserkers. Open the enclosure and wipe up the remaining forces with one quick sweep!

TAKE CONTROL OF THE GIANT'S FORGE

REQUIREMENTS: Forge a weapon capable of defeating Hel
OPTIONAL GOALS: None
ENEMIES PRESENT: Grunts, Archers, Warriors, and Berserkers

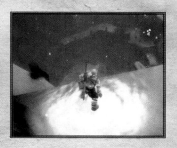

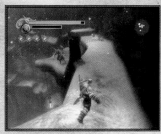

The ramp that leads into the Giant's Forge starts on the pit's western side. Use a flame pot on the clustered enemies below as you make your way down. Leap between the sections of the ramp, and climb down the large net at the base.

Use a stealth attack against one of the two warriors you meet. Then knock the berserkers and the second warrior to their deaths. Things start to heat up after this point, because archers notice your progress. It's time to start the running game! Continue down the ramp until it ends. Look beside the bottom of the ramp to see several rocky ledges. Run off the side, drop onto the ledges, and continue until you get all the way to the bottom of the Forge.

Get behind cover and let the warriors and berserkers there come to you. Kill the berserkers first, and turn to the warriors next. Several fiery drop-offs are around the sides of the Forge. Use them for fast kills if you're in the mood for block checking.

The Forge's main door is locked, but another door across from it is open. Turn and approach that door, but don't try to leap across the gap in front of it. The distance is too wide to jump. Instead, climb onto the railing to the left and shuffle across.

On the other side of that door, stairs lead both up and down. The way up takes you to a chest with many pieces of gold. The way down soon brings you to the heart of the Forge. Drive your blade into the flame and re-forge it with the heat of Giants' magic.

You now have the power to kill the greatest of beings, living and immortal. Return to Thornvik, summon Bolthor from the Dragon Stones (if you haven't already done so), and purchase all the items you need for the last battle. Don't spare any expense. Buy special moves from the Arena if you still need any, and eat a good meal before you call the men to battle. Tonight, they dine in Valhalla!

WAR COMES TO HEL'S FORTRESS

A War of Gods and Giants, Vikings and Monsters

Size of Battle:	Epic
Number of Stages:	Three
Enemies Involved:	Everything left (but no Assassins, surprisingly)
Can You Use Dragons:	All three fight for Midgard!

Stage One

The siege's first phase features many bosses to defeat. Two champions lead the defensive forces in midfield, while three shamans summon fresh troops from atop towers throughout the area. You must kill the shamans quickly, but it isn't easy.

Approach the first champion you see, and fight five or six grunts along the way. Use finishing moves, and accrue as much elemental energy as possible. Use ice to destroy the champion without investing a lot of time. Use the Dragon Runes that fall to blast the shaman on the field's right side with dragonfire.

Drive deeper into the enemy force, building up more energy before you go after the second champion. That boss is near the farthest tower, behind most of the enemy line. Kill that champion with ice as well, and use his Dragon Runes on the shaman to the left.

That leaves the final shaman in the center, and you're already standing just under his tower. Climb up the ramp that circles the outer edge, and assassinate the shaman. Berserkers, grunts, archers, and warriors protect it. Use block checking to knock the enemies off the tower, even if the fall isn't enough to kill them outright. Kill the shaman as soon as you can. This begins the battle's second phase!

Stage Two

Your troops are breaching the outer fortress, but more Legion grunts are in the way, and three giants are behind the forces. They are the real threat.

Drive down the middle and save every bit of elemental energy you can muster. Use the most advanced lightning attacks to lay the central giant low. Might of Valhalla charged with lightning practically knocks down a giant in one shot, letting you start the button combination to finish off the beast.

Kill the first giant, and use its Dragon Runes on whichever of the two survivors is farther away. Then start toward the last boss. Get more energy when you can, and use that to defeat the third giant in direct combat. With practice, you can beat this stage of battle with amazing speed.

It's possible to save extra Dragon Runes from the first phase. Players can kill two shamans and both champions and then burn the extra shaman with dragonfire. This allows you to kill two giants with dragonfire in the second stage, but it really isn't worthwhile. The giant fights are easier and pose less risk to your troops. Just be aware that you have the choice, even if it isn't necessarily easier.

Stage Three

Your dragons blast open the stairs under the portal, and that is your final target. Rush and leap between the clashing forces, and climb the stairs. Use block checking to knock off the berserkers, warriors, and grunts on the middle tier. Repeat these tactics as you climb the second flight of steps.

The portal is at the back of the highest level, with very few guards. Kill the warriors that attack, and summon Shaman Asta. Hel can bring in more warriors while Asta tries to close the portal, but they come in alone. Use either Might of Valhalla or block checks to kill the warriors or throw them to their deaths.

Viking troops can win the day outside the fortress, but more enemies appear by the moment. It seems Hel doesn't suffer defeat lightly, and she's unwilling to relinquish this last foothold in Midgard. Let Freya send you into her redoubt. That's where this siege must truly end.

THE PATH TO VICTORY

REQUIREMENTS:	End Hel's Reign
OPTIONAL GOALS:	None
ENEMIES PRESENT:	Grunts, Archers, Warriors, Berserkers, Assassins, Shamans, and Hel

It's a long climb to the top of Hel's Tower, and dozens of her minions stand in your way. None of the Viking soldiers from the siege can come with you for this assault, but the dragons plan to circle the tower and assist anytime they get a chance. Let us begin!

Two warriors and two berserkers charge over after they survive the dragons' firebombing. It's difficult to knock these enemies off the tower, thanks to the stone teeth along the sides, but careful maneuvering makes it manageable. Try to kill the berserkers outright, and toss the warriors to their deaths afterward.

Rest until you're ready for more violence, and search for the stairs on the tower's right side. Climb them and carve through the archers at the top of the steps. Get a few extra rage crystals out of the fight if you can.

FREE HACKING!

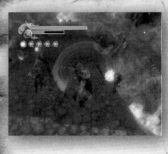

Shamans must summon most of the troops in Hel's Tower. You can use this to your advantage. Make free attacks as the enemies begin to appear, and continue slicing through the foes with slow attacks until the groups can defend themselves. You are outnumbered roughly 100-to-1, so there's no moral impetus to be even remotely fair.

isaholm ● The Path to Victory

Be more careful in the next fight. Two assassins come after you, and they're as quick as ever. Use the rage crystals that you've accrued, and don't bother saving anything for the next fight. In fact, you have time to heal after the assassins die, so just make sure you survive. Don't waste healing items or anything else of that sort.

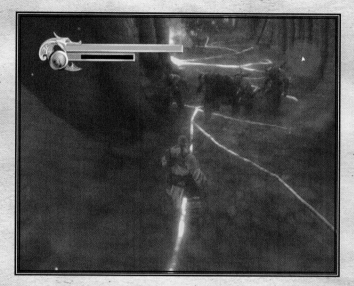

Three very large fights in succession are coming up. Each has four targets, with combinations of berserkers, grunts, and warriors. You can retreat down the hallway to heal between the fights, but you can't heal if you stay close to the action.

The fourth group you spot is mean and full of vinegar. Don't approach them while the enemies are spoiling for a fight. Just watch and see what happens. We think you'll be pleasantly surprised.

The stairs end briefly, confronting you with a long hallway with a shaman at the end. This shaman summons trios of grunts to fight in Hel's name, so make haste.

Don't get bogged down by the grunts; it gives the shaman even more time to summon. Race to the shaman's position and cut him in half before you worry about his grunts.

Resume climbing and rip through the berserkers and grunts along the way. You start to see larger fights here, but stay calm and look for ways to reduce your workload. The windows along the outer tower wall are real—you *can* knock enemies out of them. Also, you can still retreat between fights to restore your health. That makes a huge difference if you're getting beaten up and haven't refined your group-slaughtering tactics.

Always kill the dual-wielding berserkers first, then grunts, and then the heavier berserker types. Warriors go last, as usual. Use Curse of Fenrir whenever possible. This attack is great early in fights because it pushes targets away from you and knocks out weaker targets quickly.

A huge fight waits over the next bridge, and you might be too winded to survive it. Luckily, the enemies in that cluster come down with a bad case of dragonitis, so you don't have to worry about them.

However, a champion is summoned once you try to cross the bridge. Restore your health to maximum before you step onto the span, and use slow attacks to ambush the champion while he's being summoned. It's tempting to use your elemental energy here, but we suggest you hold onto it. The fighting in the tower's last chamber is even harder, and you aren't very far away now! Try to destroy the champion with conventional techniques.

A final series of assassins and mixed troops blocks the last set of steps. A shaman waits at the top, summoning as fast as it can to keep you away from its beloved mistress. Fight enemies as they appear, and don't rush ahead at first. Wait until you're high enough to see the shaman before you sprint past your enemies. Kill the shaman and finish off any stragglers. Catch your breath one more time and go after Hel directly. She's waiting for you!

Hel's chamber is divided into four sections. The fire totems she puts down erect a barrier of flame between these quadrants, making it impossible to run around the room. Meanwhile, Hel can summon grunts, warriors, and berserkers to come after you. It's a toasty place.

Destroy the fire totem that's close to you, and get your back against a wall. Stay in that defensive position to fight off the incoming Legion troops as you stay near the wall of fire. Kill enough of the enemies, and eventually the fire dies down, just for a few moments. Rush through and destroy the totem in the next quadrant. Resume a defensive position and repeat this process until all four of the totems are down.

Hel continues summoning Legion creatures to defend her for a short time, but her power to maintain the portal is fading. Soon, she uses her giant ancestry and attacks you as a mighty fire giant. Run to stay on the giant's sides and flanks.

Use any elemental energy you have to buff your weapons. Use lightning to increase your damage and tear into the giant's back again and again.

Eventually, Hel weakens and becomes susceptible to your finishing moves. This functions somewhat like an attack on a normal giant, but the final stage of actions is much longer and chains into even more complex button presses. The window for success is also shorter, so you have to press the buttons as soon as they appear.

Failure causes several new enemies to be spawns. These grunts come after you as the giant tries to recover. Kill the grunts, get back into position, and try the finishing move again.

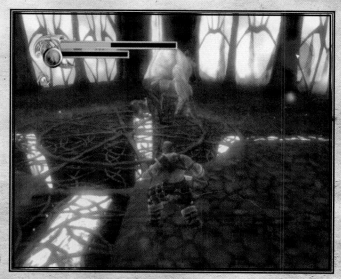

Watch what happens when the epic battle ends. You have put forth your finest effort, and the result of this conflict is fully of your making. Congratulations for all you have done!

If you played the game on Normal difficulty, it's well worth playing on Hard for further enjoyment. You can gain quite a few Achievements by beating the game's levels, as well as the campaign itself, on this more difficult setting.

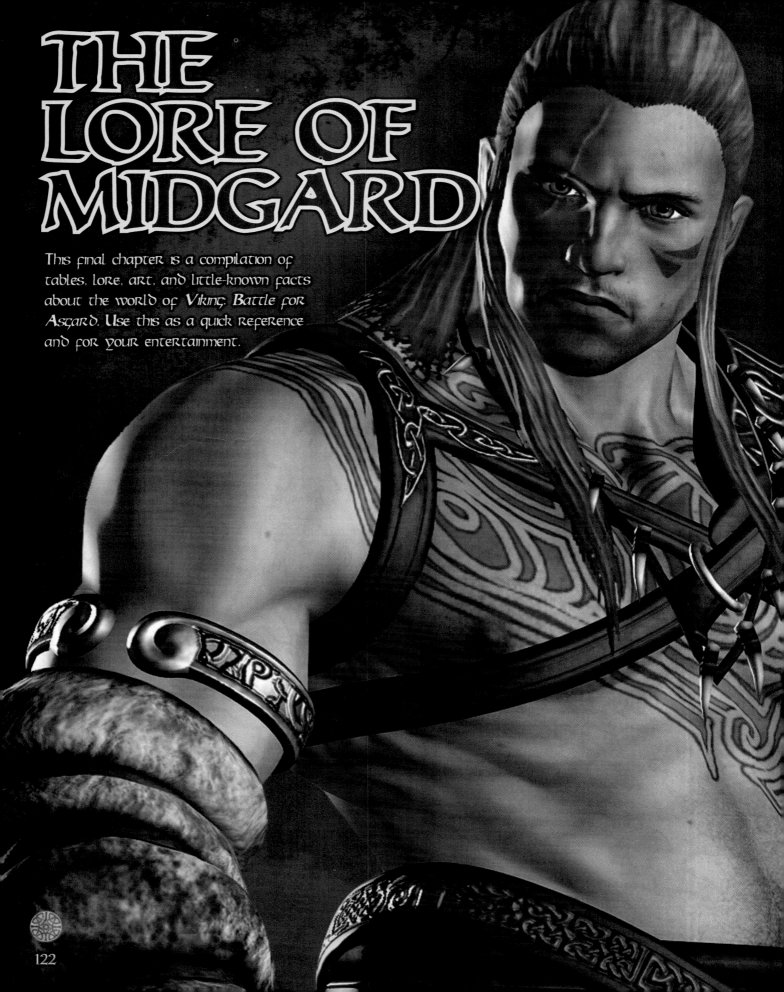

THE LORE OF MIDGARD

This final chapter is a compilation of tables, lore, art, and little-known facts about the world of *Viking: Battle for Asgard*. Use this as a quick reference and for your entertainment.

TABLE OF SPECIAL MOVES AND ELEMENTAL RUNES

ACTION	COST TO LEARN	COMMAND	EFFECT
Njord's Wrath	Free	Jump + Fast Attack	Modest-damage leaping strike
Odin's Will	150	Fast Attack followed by Slow Attack	Short stunning blow, throws enemy backward
Thor's Hammer	300	Rage Button + Slow Attack	Medium-damage strike, it leaps and slams home
Baldur's Curse	300	Rage Button + Fast Attack	Speedy lunge that nails assassins and shield users, low damage
Fenrir's Bite	700	Stealth + Slow Attack	Approach enemy suddenly and nail him for high damage
Fafnir's Might	800	Rage Button + Two Slow Attacks	Shield breaker with medium damage in a single shot
Freya's Chariot	300	Two Fast Attacks followed by a Slow Attack	Longer duration stun attack, gives Skarin more time to punish the enemy
Nidhogg's Strike	1500	Rage Button + Two Fast Attacks	Four extremely fast hits, inflicting light damage with each
Hel's Fury	1200	Jump + Slow Attack	A single, high-damage attack from the air
The Spear of Odin	500	Three Fast Attacks followed by a Slow Attack	Strong finishing move with medium damage and a stun
Valkyrie Stampede	1200	Dodge + Fast Attack	A fast reprisal when coming out of a dodge, low damage
Baldur's Silence	3000	Stealth + Close Range + Slow Attack	Delivers even more damage than Baldur's Curse
Odin's Doom	2000	Jump + Slow Attack	An upgraded version of Hel's Fury
Might of Valhalla	4000	Rage Button + Three Slow Attacks	Extremely high damage in a single strike
Valkyrie Strike	600	Four Fast Attacks followed by a Slow Attack	Difficult maneuver with high total damage and a stun
Curse of Fenrir	6000	Rage Button + Three Fast Attacks	Hits multiple targets with fast attacks
Fire Strike	240/520/760/1100	Use a Slow and a Fast Attack while charged with Fire	Can hit multiple targets, damaging them and setting them on fire
Ice Strike	260/480/800/1100	Use a Slow and a Fast Attack while charged with Ice	Freezes all targets around Skarin
Lightning Strike	250/500/840/1100	Use a Slow and a Fast Attack while charged with Lightning	Hits a single target and damages while immobilizing it

NIFLBERG STORES

Item/Rune	Price	Effect
Throwing Axe	5	Hurled at up to 25 Meters
Health Potion	30	Heals 20% of Skarin's Health
Meal	50	Adds 50% to Skarin's Health Temporarily
Gold Bag Treasure Map	190	Reveals Gold Bags on the Map
Urn Treasure Map	280	Reveals Urns on the Map
Treasure Chest Map	360	Reveals Treasure Chest on the Map
Health Advance Stage 1	420	Adds 25% to Skarin's Maximum Health
Fire Rune	240	Allows Skarin to Channel Fire
Ice Rune	260	Allows Skarin to Channel Ice
Lightning Rune	250	Allows Skarin to Channel Lightning

STORES IN GALCLIFF

Item/Rune	Price	Effect
Chieftain's Throwing Axe	8	Hurled at up to 25 Meters
Flame Pot	80	Hurled at up to 25 Meters
Health Potion	60	Heals 40% of Skarin's Health
Meal of Midgard	100	Adds 50% to Skarin's Health Temporarily
Gold Bag Treasure Map	320	Reveals Gold Bags on the Map
Urn Treasure Map	380	Reveals Urns on the Map
Treasure Chest Map	460	Reveals Treasure Chest on the Map
Health Advance Stage 1	420	Adds 25% to Skarin's Maximum Health
Health Advance Stage 2	760	Adds 25% More to Skarin's Maximum Health
Health Advance Stage 3	980	Adds 25% More to Skarin's Maximum Health
Fire Rune	240/520	Allows Skarin to Channel Fire
Ice Rune	260/480	Allows Skarin to Channel Ice
Lightning Rune	250/500	Allows Skarin to Channel Lightning

SHOPPING IN ISAHOLM

Item/Rune	Price	Effect
Axe of Odin	16	Hurled at up to 25 Meters
Flame Pot	100	Hurled at up to 25 Meters
Upgraded Health Potion	120	Heals 60% of Skarin's Health
Meal of Asgard	150	Adds 50% to Skarin's Health Temporarily
Gold Bag Treasure Map	500	Reveals Gold Bags on the Map
Urn Treasure Map	600	Reveals Urns on the Map
Treasure Chest Map	750	Reveals Treasure Chest on the Map
Health Rune Level 1	420	Adds 25% to Skarin's Health
Health Rune Level 2	760	Adds 25% More to Skarin's Health
Health Rune Level 3	980	Adds 25% More to Skarin's Health
Health Rune Level 4	1310	Adds 25% More to Skarin's Health
Fire Rune	240/520/760/1100	Allows Skarin to Channel Fire
Ice Rune	260/480/800/1100	Allows Skarin to Channel Ice
Lightning Rune	250/500/840/1100	Allows Skarin to Channel Lightning

HEROIC ACHIEVEMENTS

Name of Achievement	Point Value	Completion Goals
Viking Conqueror Normal	30	Reach the end of the game on the Normal difficulty setting
Viking Conqueror Hard	60	Reach the end of the game on the Hard difficulty setting
Niflberg Supplies Freed	20	Liberate the Farm and the Quarry in Niflberg
Dragon Summoner	15	Find and charge the dragon gem Hugin and dragon amulet, and summon a dragon
Skullbagger 1	15	Collect the 6 skulls in Darkwater
Skullbagger 2	15	Collect the 6 skulls in Holdenfort and the 6 skulls in Caldberg
Skullbagger 3	15	Collected all the skulls in Isaholm
Savior of Niflberg Normal	25	Liberate Niflberg on Normal difficulty level
Savior of Niflberg Hard	35	Liberate Niflberg on Hard difficulty level
Galcliff Supplies Freed	20	Liberate the Farm, Still, Lumber Mill, and the Quarry in Galcliff
Dragon Master	15	Complete the second dragon gem, and summon a dragon
Demon's Nemesis	40	Kill Hel's Harbinger Drakan
Redeemer of Galcliff Normal	30	Liberate Galcliff completely on the Normal difficulty level
Redeemer of Galcliff Hard	40	Liberate Galcliff completely on the Hard difficulty level
Isaholm Supplies Freed	20	Liberate the Farm, Still, Lumber Mill, and the Quarry in Isaholm
Dragon Overlord	15	Recover the final dragon gem, and summon a dragon
Death King	25	Perform 150 fatalities
Demon Eviscerator	20	Finish off 100 Legion with fatality moves
They Never Saw Me Coming	20	Execute 100 sneaky kills
Giant Killer	25	Find and slaughter a Legion Giant
The Flames of Freya	20	Buy flamepots and incinerate 10 Legion soldiers with them
Thor's Mortal Lightning Rod	5	Send a Legion back to the underworld in the most lightning-tastic way imaginable
Odin's Doomsinger	5	Use the ultimate fire attack to kill a Legion
Heimdall's Enforcer	5	Glacially wipe out a Legion using the ultimate ice attack

Name of Achievement	Point Value	Completion Goals
Deadly Axe Juggler	15	Kill 5 Legion just using throwing axes
Euthanasia Euphoria	5	Use your defensive bash to knock your Legion foes to their doom
Friend of the People	10	Power-up over 500 Vikings in your armies with runic magic
Assassin of Assassins	15	Locate and kill a Legion Assassin
Blinded to Fear	45	Kill 50 Legion without using a health potion
Viking Slaughterer	12	Learn a total of 4 new moves
Viking Butcher	10	Master the first new move at the Battle Arena
Viking Slayer	14	Master a total of 8 new moves
Viking Warrior	16	Master a total of 12 new moves
Viking Blademaster	18	Learn all the moves in the game
Demon Hacker	5	Finish off 25 Legion with fatality moves
Secretive Rogue	20	Complete the quest to sneak into Darkwater
The Perfect Killer	20	Kill a Legion Champion without being hit
Killer of Champions	5	Kill 10 Champions
Killer of Giants	5	Kill 5 Giants
Hero of Darkwater	10	Lead your army to victory at the battle for Darkwater
Hero of Holdenfort	10	Lead your army to victory at the battle for Holdenfort
Hero of Caldberg	10	Lead your army to victory at the battle for Caldberg
Hero of Thornvik	10	Lead your army to victory at the battle for Thornvik
Hero of Midgard	20	Lead your army to victory at the final battle for all Midgard
Thirst for Blood	10	Kill 50 Legion in Midgard
Lust for Blood	20	Kill 100 Legion soldiers
Champion of Champions	25	Find and defeat a Legion Champion
Berzerker	35	Kill 200 Legion soldiers
Slaughter Master	50	Kill 500 Legion soldiers
No Need for Immortality	50	Lead your army to victory at Hel's Fortress without the need for immortality.

VIKING
BATTLE FOR ASGARD
Official Strategy Guide

Written by Michael Lummis

DK/BradyGAMES, a division of Penguin Group (USA) Inc.
800 East 96th Street, 3rd Floor
Indianapolis, IN 46240

ISBN: 0-7440-1022-5

Printing Code: The rightmost double-digit number is the year of the book's printing; the rightmost single-digit number is the number of the book's printing. For example, 08-1 shows that the first printing of the book occurred in 2008.

11 10 09 08   4 3 2 1

Printed in the USA.

BRADYGAMES STAFF

PUBLISHER
David Waybright

EDITOR-IN-CHIEF
H. Leigh Davis

LICENSING MANAGER
Mike Degler

DIRECTOR OF MARKETING
Debby Neubauer

CREDITS

TITLE MANAGER
Tim Fitzpatrick

SCREENSHOT EDITOR
Michael Owen

BOOK DESIGNER
Carol Stamile

PRODUCTION DESIGNER
Bob Klunder

ACKNOWLEDGMENTS

BradyGAMES sincerely thanks everyone at Sega and The Creative Assembly. Special thanks to (in alphabetical order) Rob Bartholomew, David Bonacci, Cindy Chau, Dyna Lopez, Jim McDonagh, Wouter Van Vugt, and Katy Walden. Very special thanks to Randy Stukes, Ken Ogasawara, and Ben Harborne for your extremely professional and gracious support—we couldn't have done it without you!

Michael Lummis: My thanks to Ken Ogasawara and Randy Stukes for their help in getting the resources we needed for this guide—and to Stacey Beheler and Mike Degler too, as I'm always asking them for help getting goodies I want! With all the ice we've been getting, it's fortunate that we got the book done before Fimbulwinter set in! Thanks also to Tim Fitzpatrick for turning our material around so quickly, and to Kathleen Pleet for helping me keep my thoughts straight.